THE PROBLEM WITH
POTENTIAL

HOW TO
STOP OVERTHINKING
AND
GET OUT OF YOUR OWN WAY

JOE IGNACE

THE PROBLEM WITH
POTENTIAL

HOW TO
STOP OVERTHINKING
AND
GET OUT OF YOUR OWN WAY

JOE IGNACE

Copyright © 2023 by Joe Ignace

Book Design by Michael Trent Design

All rights reserved. No part of this publication may be reproduced, distributed, or transmitted in any form or by any means, including photocopying, recording, or other electronic or mechanical methods, without the prior written permission of the author, except in the case of brief quotations embodied in critical reviews and certain other noncommercial uses permitted by copyright law.

ISBN: 979-8-9895027-1-4

First Edition

10 9 8 7 6 5 4 3 2 1

*This book is dedicated to my wife,
who inspired me to stop procrastinating
writing this book by writing her own.*

TABLE OF CONTENTS

About the Author	3
Preface	7
Introduction	20
Chapter 1: The Problem with Potential	41
Chapter 2: Why the World Needs You to Reach Your Potential	63
Chapter 3: The Fallacy of Proficiency	77
Chapter 4: The Law of Diminishing Potential	103
Chapter 5: Identity Inspires Action	125
Chapter 6: Overcome the Cynic Within	143
Chapter 7: The Subconscious Power of Habits	159
Chapter 8: The Pain Paradox	167
Chapter 9: The Hierarchy of Friendships	177
Chapter 10: The Butterfly Effect	195
Chapter 11: Success Begins with Belief	209
Chapter 12: The Comfort Paradox	229
Chapter 13: The Power of Courage	239
Chapter 14: The Power of Purpose	265
Chapter 15: The Growth Curve	275
Conclusion	287
Author's Note	289

ABOUT THE AUTHOR

I was born in Glasgow Scotland in the United Kingdom. My family is originally from Fort Wayne, Indiana, and I spent most of my time growing up in Johnson City, Tennessee in the Easternmost part of the state. I grew up in a family of six kids, five boys and a girl. I was the third oldest and directly in the middle of all the kids. My family life was nurturing, stable, and loving throughout childhood. I am eternally grateful to have had two incredible parents who gave me an extremely good example of a loving and lasting marriage.

I attended Daniel Boone High School in Gray, Tennessee. After graduating in 2015, I attended the University of Tennessee, Knoxville where I graduated college early in December 2019 with a 3.99 GPA and a degree in accounting and a collateral in finance. My very first job outside of fast food was selling books door-to-door with a company called Southwestern Advantage. As a student, I was one of the top college students in my summers, making a combined total of $100,000 in just thirty-six weeks in my college summers traveling to areas I had never been to all over the country like Georgia, Texas, and Oklahoma. My first time leading a team as a sophomore in college, I recruited and led the twenty-fourth-best team in the entire company. I was just nineteen at the time.

After college, I spent four more summers selling books, recruiting, and leading teams totaling over 7,000 hours in just seventy-eight weeks knocking on doors. In my time at

THE PROBLEM WITH POTENTIAL

Southwestern, I was one of the top 0.5% of salespeople to ever sell at the 168 plus-year-old company. At the same time, I recruited, trained, and led sales teams to perform within the top 1% almost every year even as a teenager. I had recruited forty-three students to sell books in six years of recruiting.

At the age of twenty-four, I ran a sales force of over thirty-five sales reps representing over $1.2 million in revenue. I had the skills to knock on doors anywhere in the country and start a successful business. During that summer sales season, in just eleven weeks, I had personally built a $200,000-plus business selling educational books and apps to families in their homes while managing my team. I learned how to motivate a group of eighteen-to-twenty-three-year-olds to work over eighty hours per week in states they had never been to where their success would be based solely on their personal sales production doing something they'd never done before. I am proud to say I was able to help these young people, most of whom were college students, grow immensely and make an incredible amount of money to graduate as close to debt-free as possible.

Aside from my business accolades, the most important decision I ever made was just after I graduated college. I met and married the woman of my dreams, Danielle Ignace. Danielle has had one of the most profound impacts on my life. She has one of the biggest hearts for people I have ever experienced and challenges me to be the best man I can be daily. She encourages my faith and requires nothing but the best of me. She inspired me to write this book after she wrote

ABOUT THE AUTHOR

her first book, *Lily's Story*. She is the founder and president of the Lily's Story Foundation, which supports kids in the foster care system through continuous donations of all the proceeds from the sales of *Lily's Story*. We live happily in Knoxville, Tennessee, spending much of our time together with family and friends, being outdoors, exercising, and supporting our local community.

I own several businesses, including the Knowledge Gap Company. I help professionals and business owners grow their businesses by improving their sales process, developing better marketing funnels, building more sustainable systems, and developing incredible personal brands. I am the founder and host of *The Knowledge Gap Podcast*, where I strive to inspire business owners to build businesses that work for them (rather than the other way around).

In addition to my business, I am in the process of building the Knowledge Gap Foundation to help students in high school and college solve the problem of networking, purpose, and career direction so that they can be more inspired to do what inspires them and make the world a better place.

I sincerely hope that after you read this book, you will be encouraged and more motivated to grow as fast as you can in the pursuit of helping others. I also hope you learn from and enjoy reading *The Problem with Potential*. *Thank you*!

Joe Ignace

PREFACE

I want to thank you for your willingness to develop your mind and take action to better yourself. The book you are about to read took me over twenty-two months of work to put together. I was inspired to share my unique experiences in the hopes that the readers of this book would be encouraged to reach their potential in life and thus add value and help more people than they would otherwise. To do big things in life, you must focus on the small things. Therefore, I intentionally focused on experiences and internal thoughts that are often overlooked in our daily lives. These seemingly insignificant internal choices and thoughts have shaped the way I look at the world and have helped me find success at a surprisingly young age.

After reading this book, you will understand why you overthink and procrastinate in life. You will discover how to control your mind so that you can see the problems in your way. Then you will be challenged to face them. By facing your problems and overcoming them, you can open your eyes to the limitless possibilities of your potential and *act* toward your goals in life.

This book is all about challenging yourself to strengthen your character, your habits, and your philosophies so that you are excited to wake up every day motivated to live the life you have chosen for yourself. I will use my stories and experiences to illustrate these concepts to the best of my ability. This book is a collection of philosophies and convictions I've

THE PROBLEM WITH POTENTIAL

learned over the years from hundreds of different sources, all compiled in one place to cut to the chase and give you as much pertinent real-world application as possible. If you pick just one chapter and meditate on that chapter, applying the principles discussed, it will take you months to train your brain to break past its years of programming. My hope and prayer is that you *solve* the problem with potential in your own life and that you take ownership and share these principles and strategies with those around you. By the end of this book, you will know what the problems with potential are, and you will be equipped with foundational tools to tackle the mental blocks in your mind. You will be more self-aware of your flaws and misconceptions that cause you to overthink and procrastinate, and you will better understand what direction you want to go in life.

Potential is a word that is thrown around about young people who have a spark of talent. When potential is seen in someone, it is meant as a compliment to encourage them to be who they can become. Unfortunately, there is a point in life that most people stop believing they have potential. They erroneously believe they weren't born with the right characteristics to live out their biggest dreams. Because of this, they begin to make choices that limit their potential, and they begin limiting the potential of the people around them unintentionally. This phenomenon, called mediocrity, only occurs when people avoid their problems instead of facing them head-on.

PREFACE

EVERYONE HAS POTENTIAL

Everyone has potential. Everyone has problems. The choices you make either feed your potential—which will turn into extraordinary results—or you make choices that feed your problems. These problems will ultimately eat away at your potential, causing unintended limitations upon your future. Just like moving into a brand-new house has limitless possibilities, it also comes with problems. If you have water damage and never fix the problem, the limitlessness of the new house becomes drowned out by the incessant problems that the water damage is causing. To fix the problem, you must go through a series of painstakingly annoying and frustrating steps that can last for weeks or even months of repairs! Not to mention the thousands of dollars severe water damage can cost. Conversely, damage left untreated will deteriorate the house from the inside out. When you decide to deal with the water damage—although there is painful work and a lot of time required to fix the problem—the rot stops and the house will be safer and more secure. Instead of being constantly shackled by the thought of the water damage becoming worse, you are set free from that problem with potential. It is the same for human beings; you have incredible potential and, like everyone else, you have problems that can hold you back in life. Just like water damage in a house, your problems have the potential to grow if not dealt with. That is why you need to face them head-on, no matter what the cost. Once you face and conquer them, they have very little hold over your trajectory of success in life.

THE PROBLEM WITH POTENTIAL

Everyone in this world has limitless potential, and my goal is to help people turn their limitless potential into extraordinary results by facing their negative and potentially life-altering problems head-on. The goal is to become self-aware of your strengths and weaknesses that manifest as your successes and recurring problems. You can optimize both to work for you, rather than against you.

Facing your problems and unlocking your potential isn't easy. Not only are there internal problems that you are born with, but there are also external influences that can create new problems and make your current problems grow faster. Just like how a toxic friend group can influence you to think more negatively about life, the people you surround yourself with have a massive positive or negative effect on reaching your potential.

Before this book, you were probably told that you can only do "so much." You have certain limitations, and you need to accept them. While acceptance of flaws and natural weaknesses is valuable for self-awareness, acceptance does not mean that you cannot achieve great things in your life no matter the weaknesses or setbacks you may have.

PREFACE

THE STORY OF ETHELDA BLEIBTREY

In 1920, Ethelda Bleibtrey was the first American woman to win an Olympic gold medal for swimming. She was a star of the Antwerp Olympics, and that same year she also became the first woman to win *three gold medal*s in swimming. She was unstoppable. What most people don't know about Bleibtrey is that she was diagnosed with polio at fifteen-years-old. Polio's cure wasn't found until 1955, and the effects of the disease were terrible. Polio can cause paralysis and can affect the arms or legs. Despite this major uncontrollable in her life, she persisted in swimming her entire life to counteract the negative effects of the virus and is now an inspiration and a lesson to us all.

At age fifteen, Bleibtrey was told by prominent and trustworthy doctors that she would lose movement and control of her limbs. Bleibtrey had no business disagreeing with them, but she did. She wanted a different life than what she was being prescribed. Through the excruciating pain of constant therapy, she decided to live a life she wanted to live regardless of what people told her.[1] Her potential to succeed was determined by her conscious decision to face her problems head-on. No one can decide your potential other than you and God.

---

1 Britannica, T. Editors of Encyclopaedia. *Ethelda Bleibtrey*. (2023, May 2). Encyclopedia Britannica. https://www.britannica.com/biography/Ethelda-Bleibtrey

THE PROBLEM WITH POTENTIAL

Like Bleibtrey, you have also been told what is possible and what is impossible for you to achieve. What you've been told likely isn't true. It's based on the presupposition and the mental belief barrier of the person who told you that you can't do something. What's rare for some doesn't have to be rare for you, and I believe that there is tremendous potential in every human being on the planet. With the right mindset, mentors, and direction, you can achieve incredible results. Instead of making the statement "there's no way," I want you to ask yourself, "why not me?"

Whether you ever receive a gold medal from the Olympic Games, start a billion-dollar business, or simply volunteer at your local church, all I care about is that you become the best version of yourself and reach your full potential.

YOUR POTENTIAL IS IN THE BALANCE

Your potential to achieve what you can achieve balances on a razor's edge. While some problems—like polio for Bleibtrey—can never be fully resolved, you can still reach your potential by focusing on doing your absolute best. Like Bleibtrey, who was dealt a bad hand that meant she had to overcome substantially more physical setbacks than her swimming competitors, you can overcome your seemingly insurmountable problems and avoid the mental prison of mediocrity by setting goals for your life based on your willingness to learn and your work ethic. Your past mistakes, labels,

PREFACE

and failures do not determine your future. Your personal choices determine your future.

Your potential is malleable for good or for evil. Your potential is limitless in the sense that nothing can hold you back from doing big things. Through procrastination you can create self-imposed limits to your potential. You either use your time to turn your potential into extraordinary results that manifest in the real world, changing the lives of many to essentially "reach your true potential," or you can avoid the problems that hold you back in life, thus nullifying the effectiveness of your God-given talents.

In this book, you will be confronted with some of the most common problems that nearly every human being faces that hold them back from becoming the best version of themselves. You will examine your personal mindset and motivations to learn how to motivate yourself and face your problems internally. You will also learn about the external effects of those around you and how to control your external environment and social circles so that you will be influenced and encouraged to be the best version of yourself in the pursuit of helping others.

If you are willing to face these internal and external problems, you will be working towards reaching your full potential: where you can do the things you've always dreamt of; where you are an unstoppable force of nature; where you help countless others even if you never personally meet them.

THE PROBLEM WITH POTENTIAL

My goal is that you fall in love with challenging the status quo of mediocrity and that you begin to feel empowered to overcome your problems even if you never thought they were impossible to overcome. I want to see you break your internal belief barriers—the negative thoughts that tell you, "You can't do that," or "You're not good enough,"—by helping you realize that your goals are possible regardless of where you start. The only thing holding you back from your goals is understanding how to reach them, which always starts with first believing that you can achieve them. I would love to see you shatter the glass ceiling that every human being creates in their mind based on past and often painful failures that limit them to the lowest of their potential. I want to inspire you to grow past the shackles of learned mediocre normalcy and instead see the world in a drastically different and exciting way with challenges to overcome. I want you to solve YOUR problem with potential.

THE HELPING OTHERS FOCUS

The Problem with Potential is all about helping you learn how to achieve your greatest results in life by helping you understand how to internally and externally motivate yourself through reflecting and analyzing your perspective on life, how you think, and who you surround yourself with. This book is designed to inspire ACTION, as simply talking about things never truly changes much. This book is all about encouraging

PREFACE

you to do what you've always wanted to do by explaining that the only reason you haven't done it yet is because of overthinking. This is not a get-rich-quick book or a self-help book. This book is a LONG-TERM personal growth book that is much closer to a helping-others book because by you reaching your potential in life, the results you achieve will inspire others to do the same. Helping others in the case of reaching your potential is not only a secondary benefit to reaching your potential, but it is also a necessary component to reach your potential. ***Without being motivated by helping others, you can never truly become the best version of yourself.*** If you are only motivated by personal gain, you are limiting yourself by avoiding personal sacrifice and the responsibility to make meaningful changes within yourself that would benefit others. Naturally, you would become more egotistical, selfish, and uninfluential. But that's not who you truly are, nor is that where your true potential will lead. It is the constant problem with potential that we all share.

The fight between self and selflessness is constant when reaching your potential. Another reason you need to focus on helping others is that maintaining the motivation to solve your problem with potential is paradoxical. Meaning, the only way to truly reach *your* potential is by being motivated by the pursuit of helping *others*. To reach your personal goals, you have to help other people reach their goals as well. One cannot happen without the other. Without the desire to help others, there is a point in everyone's growth journey where becoming the best version of yourself will be too costly for your personal gain. There will be a moment when you will want to quit, where the next step in your growth journey is so difficult and painful that, if only motivated by your own internal goals, you will give up. At that moment, the one thing that will push you past this difficult wall is the pursuit of helping others and realizing that a better you can help more people. Without the desire to help others, you will be limited and—like many potentially great people before you—put off becoming the best version of yourself.

In life, the most precious resource is time because your time is limited and you can never replace it. Therefore, the most important investment of your time is developing yourself to be a servant-hearted leader. Your personal limits also limit the impact you will have on the world and determine how much value you add to others. Your mind is the most important thing to develop, for it is the lens through which you see life. It is where everything in your life, good or bad, will be created. Your mind can never truly be taken from you.

We are on a journey together and this book is about helping others. I will give many examples of utter failure from my life and others that turned into explosive growth to help you understand that becoming successful and becoming the person you want to be isn't easy, but it is possible. Personal growth is the most difficult endeavor one can undertake. It is also the MOST IMPORTANT path one must travel. Suppose

PREFACE

you don't grow and learn to live life loving the process of growth. In that case, you will be perpetually unhappy with the results of your life because outcomes such as money, status, cars, fame, and professional success will never make you truly happy. If you can't be happy with $100, you'll never be happy with $1,000,000. Living a life in pursuit of "happiness" is a losing game because the target will always be moving. Why? Happiness is based on a dopamine release in the brain that has to increase to keep you feeling high. The pursuit of personal growth is a pursuit of joy. Joy is a state of being content. Contentment is a state of thankfulness. Thankfulness is being grateful for what you do have and what you can control while not worrying about what you can't control. Gratitude isn't about comparison; it's about the lack thereof. Gratitude is the realization that you are uniquely designed for a purpose and that is all you need to be. You don't have to be somebody else. There is nothing inherently wrong with who you were made to be, but rather always try to grow and realize your potential so that you can help more people. Gratitude is about knowing that you are doing your best with the talents and resources you currently have as you attempt to add value to others and the world. When you let go of worrying about the uncontrollable, you can find joy in doing your best in pursuing personal growth and helping others.

THE DEFINITION OF SUCCESS

In modern culture, success is often equated with becoming rich and famous. The idea is that those who have many material things and affluential success are by definition successful. I reject this simplistic view of success. For example, if you come to your riches but help very few people, are you successful? Take the tobacco industry, for example. According to the World Health Organization, "Tobacco kills up to half of its users. Tobacco kills more than 8-million people each year, including 1.3 million non-smokers who are exposed to secondhand smoke."[2] According to Statista, the tobacco industry generated $941.1 billion in revenue worldwide in 2023.[3] Are the people who run these companies truly successful? Yes, they make a lot of money and probably have nice houses, cars, and fame within their social circles. But are they adding or subtracting value to people? The problem with organizations that produce and distribute tobacco that kills millions is that their definition of success is based on financial success. When you make financial success your definition of success, whether you add value to or harm others becomes less important to you than money and pursing the most profit possible. If money is more important than people, then you don't bat an eyelash

---

[2] *Tobacco.* (2023, July 31). World Health Organization. https://www.who.int/news-room/fact-sheets/detail/tobacco

[3] *Tobacco Products - Worldwide: Statista Market Forecast.* (n.d.). Statista. https://tinyurl.com/tobaccoproductsworldwide

PREFACE

at a combined 9.3 million deaths a year due to your product because at least you made $941.1 billion in revenue.[4]

True success is realized in helping others, and to reach your greatest potential, you must first realize that material possessions are less valuable than human beings. Money is a byproduct of helping others and adding value to the world. The more value you add, the more people you help, and the more money you make.

Money and notoriety are not the end goals of life; the goal is to solve problems for others and make the world a better place. In doing this, you will end up well off whether you start a nonprofit, start a Fortune 500 company, or volunteer in your local community.

There are much bigger problems in the world that need to be tackled rather than achieving personal materialistic success. Being wealthy and doing well financially is by no means wrong! I would argue you can impact a larger group of people if you do well with your financial success, but you have to focus on helping others as your mission or wealth will tempt you into selfishness.

There is much more to life than money, fame, and cars. The true measure of success in life is how many people you have impacted positively, not how much wealth you have

---

4 World Health Organization. (2023, July 31). *Tobacco.*

created for yourself. There are people in this world who need someone who is motivated to make a difference, to help those who can't help themselves. They need someone to stand up and devote their time, treasure, and talents to make the world a better place. And who better to take part in this than you? I believe God has a plan for your life, and if you look hard enough, you just might see where to go.

Remember as you are reading about facing your problems and realizing your potential, others will see you grow and you might just be the inspiration they need to do the same. The antidote to procrastination and overthinking and the solution to the problem with potential is always *action*.

As you read, you will be promoted to partake in multiple exercises designed to help you organize your thoughts about topics I bring up throughout the book. I've created a free PDF workbook for you to use as a companion to your reading because it's not about what you know, it's about how you apply it. And I hope this will help you apply what you read to make a massive impact on your life. Just scan the QR code below, click on *The Problem with Potential Workbook (free)*, fill in your information so we can stay in contact, and you'll be emailed your very own workbook to get the most out of this experience.

 Scan the QR code below or go to **https://joeignace.com/theproblemwithpotentialworkbook** for your free workbook download.

Good luck!

INTRODUCTION

In the fall of 2015, I had just started my freshman year in college, and like many students, I didn't have a car. I grew up in a family with six kids including myself, so personally affording a car at sixteen wasn't really an option as I had only worked part-time at Dairy Queen and a couple of other small jobs. Instead of having my own car, my brothers and I all shared a 1999 Ford pickup truck with over 200,000 miles on it throughout high school. It was one of those trucks with a really big bed and rear-wheel drive and only one bench to sit on that could barely fit three people. For two years I sat squished between my two bigger and older brothers on the way to school every morning and on the way home every afternoon. After turning sixteen, I drove that lovely truck every day until graduation. It was clear that this truck would be the "hand me down" vehicle, so I would be heading to college without a car.

So, with very little discretionary money, I brought a bike instead. That bike got destroyed by some vandals on campus about a month in, and so I was a walker through my freshman semesters. By mid-spring of 2016, I was doing well in school, and I had signed up for a summer internship opportunity out of state, and so I asked my dad to help me buy a car. He agreed on the condition that I would pay him back after I had made money over the summer and found me the best car any young man could hope for. I mean, it had everything. It was stylish. It was hip. It was a 2007 deep *purple* Ford Fusion. That's right, purple. It was a beautiful car! And I needed this car because the internship that I landed was located all the way in Dallas, Texas with the Southwestern Company.

The internship with the Southwestern Company I obtained was one for the books. It was challenging. It was heroic. It was the adventure of a lifetime, a resume builder, something that would set me apart from my peers! I had signed up for a *door-to-door* summer sales internship, an internship that every young boy *dreamt* about. I mean, who doesn't want to knock on doors and sell things to strangers? And this wasn't just any door-to-door summer sales internship, it was also *lucratively* based on income based entirely on sales, with people I had just met, in a place I had never been, living with an undetermined host family, doing something I had never done, and working long hours. I was told the most successful dealers worked more than 80 hours each week. Did I mention that expenses were all on me and there were *absolutely* no guarantees? What a dream, right?

You may be asking yourself: how did this happen? Quite simply, there weren't a lot of internship opportunities for a college freshman at the time, and I didn't want to work a dead-end summer job back at my local Dairy Queen in Gray, Tennessee. I wanted to make more money than possible at most part-time jobs to pay for school and pay off the debt I had accrued living on campus my freshman year. The average student made over $8,000 at this particular internship in just under twelve weeks. The only catch was that I

INTRODUCTION

was paid solely for my production, and if I wanted to do well, I would have to work eighty hours a week to build a profitable business worth the time. Despite this, I decided to challenge myself by selling books door-to-door. I wanted to prove I could do anything I put my mind to.

Once I accepted the internship, I did what all normal college students did, and I decided to procrastinate all of my preparation until the week before sales school. I prioritized everything else ahead of this internship, which at the time made sense. In hindsight, I would not recommend spreading yourself this thin and procrastinating preparing for one of the hardest things you could do. But alas, you live, and you learn.

Thus, the summer was approaching quickly, and I crammed for my finals and then I crammed for my 80-hour-a-week summer door-to-door sales internship. Needless to say, I was unprepared when I got to sales school.

Sales school was an *intense* weeklong program that whipped me right into shape, similar to what I would assume boot camp feels like. The whole point of sales school was to emulate the schedule and mindset of the company's top 2% of salespeople. Previously, selling in the top 2% took at least 80 hours a week. I wanted to be successful, so I knew I would need to work that much or more. I had to learn to be highly structured and disciplined to do so. Deciding to do the uncomfortable thing would have to become second nature to me.

THE PROBLEM WITH POTENTIAL

So, I moved to Nashville, Tennessee for the training simulation for a week. My daily routine, and that of my fellow students, was brutal. I woke up at 5:59 each morning. My leaders told me the logic behind this was that "average people wake up at 6:00 a.m." Now, of course, not all average people wake up at 6:00 a.m. nor does waking up one minute earlier mean we are superior, but the idea behind this was designed to shift our mindsets by buying into the *Slight Edge* mentality. One extra minute each day, although not much in the short-term, adds up to nearly six hours of extra time in a year. If you were intentionally focused on developing a mentality of mental toughness, then you would be more successful at selling books.

In addition to mindset coaching, I learned how to build strong habits. For example, once the alarm rang, I was taught to quite literally soar out of bed and race to the shower to beat my three roommates to the small hotel shower to take an *ICE COLD*—and I'm not exaggerating—thirty-second shower to wake up. This may sound absolutely crazy, but as it turns out there are a lot of health and psychological benefits to this peculiar practice. And taking these freezing cold showers always woke me up faster than coffee ever could.

The basic idea behind the cold shower routine is that if you take a cold shower first thing in the morning, you've started your day doing something really *difficult*. You essentially faced the *problem* of waking up and being lethargic head-on. If you discipline yourself to start your day by facing your problems head-on, every other *disciplined* decision becomes

INTRODUCTION

easier to make in comparison. Therefore, you build the habit of doing the hardest things that are good for you, such as a cold shower, with positive health benefits, such as increasing your metabolism. Herein lies the entire purpose of this "over-the-top" internship: *developing mental toughness*.

The goal was to maximize every second of the week of sales school; therefore, so immediately after the shower, I would go grab my twenty-five-lb. book bag with my PB&J pre-packed lunch from the night before, and I would begin to prepare to sell books from the moment I left the hotel room at 6:15 a.m. until 9:00 p.m. every single day. During that time, I would either be in a conference-style training about how to sell books effectively or actively practicing what I would be saying the first week of selling books. In addition to that, every night there were teambuilding fireside chats, motivational speakers, and intense door-knocking drills to help all of the first-year students get prepared for the inevitability of the mass rejection we were all about to experience in less than seven days. By the end of the sales school experience, I had developed some incredible habits, relationships, and mentalities that I wouldn't have learned anywhere else in such a short amount of time. After training, I shot off to a new state to sell with my university's group. In my case, I was with the University of Tennessee students, and we were heading off to northern Texas.

My first summer selling books was in a small town in northern Texas called Krum. Krum was a very small town of around

THE PROBLEM WITH POTENTIAL

5,000 people. I wouldn't have called it a paradise by any means, but it was a great place to sell books because Krum was where a lot of families had settled down to raise their kids, and I was selling children's educational books, apps, and websites. Many people in Krum thought that I was wasting my time in such a small population center. I find it interesting, looking back, at all of the advice I was given about "where" I should be selling. Locals would often tell me to go to the suburbs of thousands upon thousands of manicured lawns and cookie-cutter neighborhoods to increase my chances of making sales. These people didn't understand what I was learning. I was learning that selling is much more about connecting and building community with the locals so that when I was knocking, I would be able to market myself on Facebook and through past client connections so that the total number of doors I knocked decreased based on the fact that I knew enough people in the area to be known, liked, and trusted even as a door-to-door salesman. In other words, knocking on doors in a small town meant that if I worked tremendously hard to get just a few initial customers, I would build momentum from word-of-mouth advertising, and with that momentum, there was a greater chance that the next family I talked to would be connected to another family in the town that already knew me, thus granting me connections and brand awareness I would never have achieved in a massive suburb. In my experience of spending over seven summers selling books, spending over

INTRODUCTION

7,000 hours, and talking to over 24,000 people across the country, it was rare that people knew their neighbors unless they were in smaller communities.

At the time, I was like many young men who were just starting out in life. I was eighteen and I believed I was invincible. I was also very skilled at putting on a facade to mask my true emotions. When I started selling books, I was the most nervous I had been in nearly my entire life that very first day. But, of course, I couldn't let my leaders know that. Not only was I nervous about talking to strangers and doing something I had never done before, but I was also fairly *untalented* at first.

At the very first door I knocked on I completely forgot what I was supposed to say. Keep in mind I had been practicing, word for word, what to say for the last ten days straight. Throughout that first day, I continued to fail and fail. I failed so often during my first three hours on the job that I began to question if I even knew how to speak correctly. Eventually one of my managers came to work with me, and I kind of "sold" some books to someone who didn't have a job, wasn't in high school or any form of education, and didn't have any money. I will say that it felt pretty amazing that someone would spend twenty minutes with me to hear about what I was doing, look at the books I was selling, and "order" something from me. I also thought to myself, how does someone buy educational resources if they can't use the product or provide money for it? I realized that not only was the sale solidified on some pretty shaky ground, but during the sign-up process, I had forgotten how to fill out an order form as well. So, my "sale" took much longer than it was supposed to, which caused me to panic and rush myself to get finished as fast as possible. I was so focused on writing up the order correctly, that I wasn't even worried about getting any money and completely forgot to collect any sort of payment. So, when he promised to pay me at the end of the summer for the books, I was naïve enough to believe him. I later learned that if the prospect didn't give you any money, it really wasn't a sale even if they signed off on it, because if there is no down payment, people don't often remember that they even ordered something from you.

The good news was that at the same time that I was experiencing immense failure, I was also very motivated. I was stubborn and unshakable, so I just kept going regardless of any and all rejection. Besides, I didn't have anything better to do. After all, I was 3,000 miles from my home back in Knoxville, Tennessee. So, I kept going, and I kept hearing nos. I kept making absolutely no money.

On my second day, the "worst-case scenario" happened to me. I would later learn through life experience and developing a larger perspective on life that this moment wasn't exactly the "worst-case" scenario, but at that time, it was extremely frustrating, all things considered.

I was working on the outskirts of my little town, talking to a bunch of well-mannered farmers, and on this particular

INTRODUCTION

morning, I had my manager, Zac, showing me the ropes. I remember pulling into a gravel driveway in the country to knock on someone's door. It was a sunny morning, and the birds were chirping. We were in God's country, Texas. I pull up to the house, knock... and knock once again... No answer. So, I went back to my car to go to the next one. I started my car to leave the property, I made a crucial error; I attempted to show off my macho driving skills by whipping the car out of the driveway to impress my passenger. Without much thought, I hit the gas hard. As I was whipping the car out of the driveway, I seemed to misplace a large green cattle fence in my mirror on the left side of the car and slammed and scraped the entire left side of my vehicle into the lime-green fence. SCREEEEEEEECH. I heard a slow release of air from my back left tire. I immediately pulled forward to get unstuck, making the massive dent and scratched paint job even worse. I heard the last gasps of air leaving my back left tire as my car flattened to the earth. In my mind, my life had just ended. This was my perceived "worst-case scenario."

Of course, there are a multitude of *worse* worst-case scenarios that could have happened. but like most people, during this moment, I blew this mistake up into what I *perceived* to be a *worst-case scenario*. I had a poor perspective on the situation. My internal fears and inadequacies flared up, and I started to attack myself for being a failure. Keep in mind that at this point in the summer, I had made nearly no money and had spent nearly two weeks doing this

THE PROBLEM WITH POTENTIAL

very difficult internship that 30% of people quit within the first three weeks. I was pretty confident that I was at the near bottom of the pack my first few days as well as my first two weeks. I was putting a lot of pressure on myself to succeed at something I had never really done before, but I wanted to prove to myself that I could do this. I perceived success.

At this moment, the only reason I didn't flip out with utter frustration was the fact that there was another human being with me, watching me for the day. I remember Zac getting out of the car with a big smile.

Zac had sold with the Southwestern Company for seven summers already. Every person I had met who had spent this much time selling door-to-door was ALWAYS smiling. No amount of rejection, mishaps, or mistakes could break this man's unshakably optimistic attitude.

After he stood up and took stock of the situation, he said, "No worries; do you know how to change a tire?" I told him, "No," and he asked if I had a car jack. He said it was actually pretty simple, and he'd show me if we had the tools. Unfortunately, I hadn't packed a car jack. Back then, I didn't know much about cars. Weirdly enough, we ended up borrowing a car jack from the homeowner whose driveway we were stuck in and whose fence I had damaged, but they didn't care that much. Upon closer inspection, the fence did way more damage to my car than my car had done to the fence. So, we were able to get the spare tire on in a timely fashion, and then, we just went to the next door.

INTRODUCTION

From this point on, while Zac was with me, I had a constant scowl and angry look on my face. I was really angry with myself for making such a boneheaded decision. I was angry about the financial loss I incurred with my car. I just didn't want to be doing this anymore, and all I wanted to do was take a break. Obviously, sales didn't go that well for the next two hours. At around 12:30 p.m., Zac asked me to drop him off at his car so he could go help another first-year salesperson just like he was helping me for the second half of the day. As we were driving to his car, he proceeded to tell me a story that changed my life.

Zac shared a story of his best week ever from a couple of summers ago. He started the story with a big smile and a lot of enthusiasm. He was really proud to have accomplished his best week, as it took him five years of selling books to achieve his best week ever. You would be proud too if you could make $5,000 in a week selling books.

He was telling me this story about how he felt unstoppable. Everyone was buying, and the job was so easy for him that week. I didn't relate one bit at that moment, but then he started describing how his knee was bothering him throughout his best week. At some point during the week, his knee had popped while he was getting out of his car, and it was swelling pretty badly towards the end of the week. That was a long time to be up on a swollen knee carrying a heavy bag of sample books. But he was telling me about how he

THE PROBLEM WITH POTENTIAL

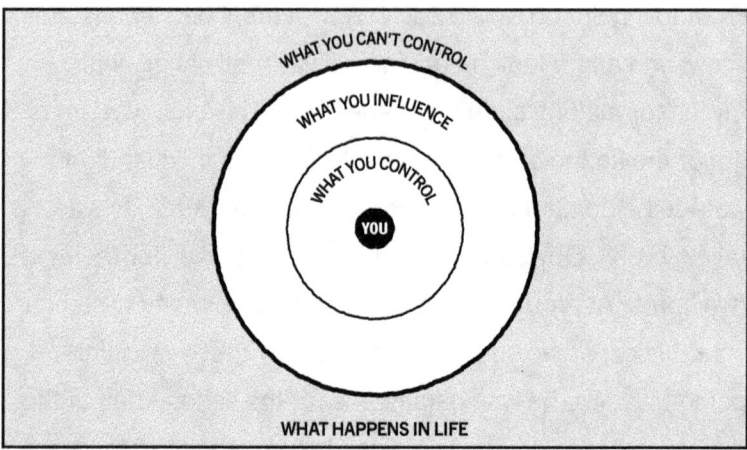

Figure 0.1: This figure represents the vastness of uncontrollables in life along with the few things you can influence, and the even fewer things you can control.

had such a good attitude regardless of his knee. And every time one of his prospects would ask him about his knee, he would just prop it up on the couch or an extra chair and keep giving everyone his best. After he finished selling for the week, he decided to go to urgent care just to make sure his knee was okay. As it turned out, he tore his MCL on Monday of his best week ever. He had a torn MCL and had his best week in sales of his entire life. Regardless of his knee, he had given that week his personal best, and no outward circumstances could bring him down. Without him directly telling me about how I was focusing on my external circumstances and being too hard on myself, I immediately understood the analogy. I had a popped tire and it ruined my day. My mind and my body were totally fine, and I was in no physical pain. I was allowing my temporary external circumstances to dictate my internal feelings and motivations. This had to stop.

INTRODUCTION

He explained that life is 10% what happens to you and 90% about how you react to it. Every time a tough day comes at you, you either let it beat you and try to forget that day ever existed, or you turn that "bad circumstance" into an incredible overcomer story that you'll tell your kids and your grandkids for the rest of your life. The idea is that you have the choice to decide your reaction to your circumstances no matter how good or bad they are. The choice is internal, and the choice to do your best has been made by countless individuals regardless of their past mistakes and failures. And from Zac's story, this was the first time in my life that I realized that no matter how bad I perceived my particular set of circumstances currently were, there has been and always will be someone who had it worse and decided to do their best rather than feel sorry for a past mistake, failure, or inadequacy. Instead, they faced their problems head-on and thus produced a result that they could look back on and be proud of. They focused on competing with themselves and decided to reach their potential rather than limit themselves by finding every reason why they couldn't succeed. My success and happiness had nothing to do with my results but rather my personal growth.

This example called me out of my victimhood mentality. External circumstances don't determine joy, peace, or happiness but rather internal perspective and motivation. I stopped trying to be like everyone else—who at the time was outselling me—and I focused on becoming the best version of myself, which meant trusting in God, treating people well, and making the world a better place. I wanted to inspire the families I was speaking with to believe in themselves and think bigger than they had previously thought possible. I wanted to see these students believe that they could do anything they put their minds to. The secret to reaching my potential was taking personal responsibility for my life by actively improving my mindset and character by competing with myself rather than comparing myself to those around me. I realized that the choice to become the best version of myself is completely up to me and that no one can decide how I will react to my circumstances but me.

Looking back on the experience of my "supposed" worst-case scenario, I realized that often when "bad" things happen, they only have power over you when you allow the circumstance to blind you from seeing the bigger picture in life and instead hyper-focus on the present mistakes you are currently making. In fact, before this moment I had allowed certain failures and unfavorable situations to ruin my day, week, and sometimes even months by lacking the proper perspective.

What is so interesting is that popping my tire on my second week and making nearly no sales was about the *BEST* thing that could've happened to me. I wasn't hurt, I wasn't robbed, I wasn't stuck in a pit somewhere. But I was angry at myself for making the mistake. And talking to Zac at that crucial moment of frustration where I had, in the past, habitually allowed

INTRODUCTION

frustration to rule over me, HAD to happen. I *needed* to face my problem of self-doubt, self-loathing, and self-destruction as soon as possible or I would never have gotten on the path to my true potential. I would have internally talked myself out of becoming the best version of myself, for if I had allowed my worst thoughts about myself being not good enough to overtake me, I would have eventually ruined my confidence in my ability to achieve even the smallest of tasks, resulting in the decision of procrastinating in facing my problems.

Many of life's questions and choices about success are analogous to the rules for success of a summer selling books door-to-door. Whether you are stepping out of your comfort zone to sell something, change jobs, or sing in public, the same feelings of inferiority, insecurity, and fear of failure show up unless you've faced them. And even if you've faced these fears and insecurities, they can still show up before you can accomplish what you set yourself out to do. The only difference in achieving what you are striving for is that you are stronger after facing your problems and therefore accomplish what you set out to do.

What if you *start* and *fail*, and it just doesn't work out for you? What if it doesn't come easily? *What if you're not good enough?* These questions confront every one of us, and our responses to these questions determine whether we reach our potential and achieve our dreams or not. Your external

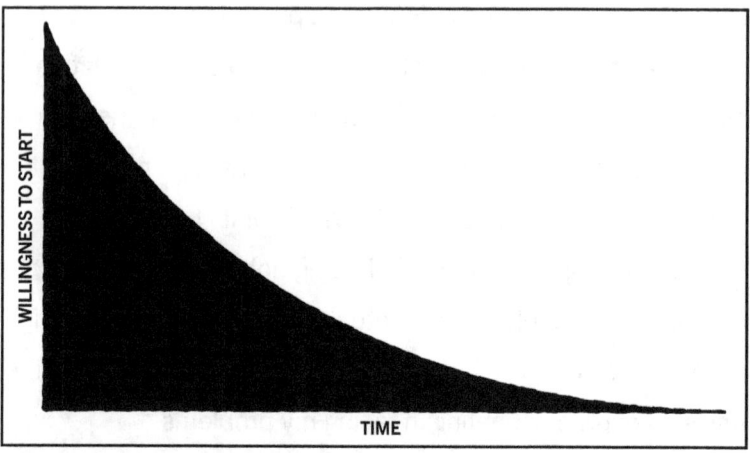

Figure 0.2: The more you procrastinate, or the longer you wait, the less willing you are to start something.

circumstances don't determine your decision to face your problems and overcome your emotions; they are but a test that reflects your internal thoughts and motivations.

I had popped my tire, had made nearly no money to get it fixed, and spent nearly two weeks doing an internship that 30% of people quit within the first three weeks. But at the end of all of that… I was totally okay.

I could walk. I could talk. I wasn't injured. I realized that even if my current perceived "worst-case scenario" does occur, I would be completely okay, and life would go on. Even if I fail, it's not the end of the world. The fear of failure had left me because it had happened! When I did fail in the short-term, I felt more at peace because… well, it couldn't get any worse, right? I was just fine. It was uncomfortable, but without the

INTRODUCTION

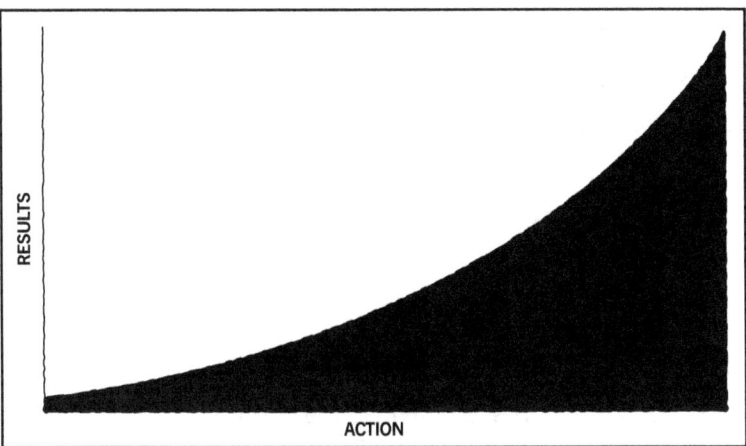

Figure 0.3: As you take action, you see results. The more action you take the more results you see, and the more action you will be willing to take.

failure to prove to myself that it wasn't a big deal, I would never have come to this conclusion. This is why you need to face your problems head-on to unlock your potential.

During this story, that spans maybe ten minutes when I was just eighteen, I had the epiphany that your mindset is everything. I realized that I had heard this a million times before, but I never really knew what it meant until the moment that I EXPERIENCED it. It wasn't until I was in a state of complete failure and frustration that this happened. This is the only way it really could happen, and I am so thankful for the failure that led me to this realization. And this is why you need to put yourself in places where you develop a tougher mindset in order to grow.

As I was having this epiphany, Zac's story ended. He smiled at me and told me to go give it my all and to *make a good*

THE PROBLEM WITH POTENTIAL

story. He got out of my car, and I was met with silence and my own thoughts. You can't "think" yourself into overcoming your problems; you have to act. If you are inactive and "think" for too long, you will overthink. You will "think" yourself out of doing the hard thing because your mind wants to avoid the pain of facing your problems at all costs. So, instead of thinking about anything, I immediately decided to go make a good story that I would be proud of. I didn't hesitate or allow my negative thoughts to convince me to quit.

I drove back to the area I was knocking, and I worked the entirety of the rest of the day until 9:40 p.m. I had no sales until, finally, my last two doors. Incredibly, both families bought from me, one right after the other! The sales success were right at the finish line. Could you imagine what would've happened if I had called it quits a mere thirty minutes earlier in the day and given up on it? What if I had given in to my thoughts of "this won't work" when it was nearly dark outside? Instead, I just kept going until I couldn't go anymore.

I didn't make a ton of money that day. I probably only made $100 for over twelve hours of work, but I did finish strong. I experienced a confidence anchor, which is a moment that I can look back on that proves I can push through my problems. This same moment has and will continue to give me confidence for the rest of my life. I made a good story, and I am so lucky to have been taught this lesson when I was just eighteen years old. Because if I could face this

INTRODUCTION

one difficult moment, then I could face other really hard moments, and I can bet on myself to push through even if I don't feel like it.

There will be many difficult problems, mistakes, and difficult circumstances in life than a single popped tire, and in order to face them, you have to start somewhere. Where you start doesn't matter; what matters is that you don't procrastinate and just start. Your future self will thank you. I believe that God has a plan for your life, and you have an integral role to play in making the world a better place.

The lesson I learned that day is worth more than all four years of my college career. It is that you have two choices in life. You can allow your internal negative problematic thoughts and your external problematic circumstances to drown out your potential for greatness, or you can decide to conquer your problems and unlock your potential to do big things in this world. It is completely up to you, and no one can make the decision for you.

This story is the basis of this entire book. I can only imagine what kind of person I would be today if I didn't buy into the mentality that your attitude is everything. As you read through this book, just remember, that you can make a heaven of hell, or a hell of heaven and it all starts within your own mind.

CHAPTER 1

THE PROBLEM WITH POTENTIAL

Potential is great. Action is better. Everyone has potential, but few achieve anything with it. Be the few.

There are two problems with potential. First, problems in your life have the potential to get A LOT worse; and secondly, leaving everything to "potentially" happen will be the death of your success. Those with "great potential" should take this as a compliment while young and an insult when they are older. If you still have potential, then you haven't achieved that which you are capable of. Ask yourself, why? Why haven't you exhausted your potential and reached your absolute best results yet? Why haven't you pushed yourself to be the best version of yourself to add value to the world? Or currently,

THE PROBLEM WITH POTENTIAL

why aren't you working towards realizing your potential by achieving what you are fully capable of?

So many incredibly talented and wonderfully unique people limit themselves from accomplishing what they are truly capable of doing. How many people have you heard sing with a quite angelic voice but are afraid to sing in front of even three people? Or how many people refrain from offering to help someone because they don't feel good enough, even though they have the answer to their problem? Or what about all the people who have dream jobs but resign themselves to working a job they hate out of fear of failure?

Herein lies the problem with potential. If you have untapped potential, you are likely allowing your PROBLEMS to hold you back from reaching your potential. Here lies the important relationship with your unsolved problems, issues, demons, and your success. They are directly correlated. When one goes up, the other goes down. When you allow your problems to consume your life through avoidance, your potential for success shrinks and becomes limited. When you face your problems head-on, you are minimizing them, solving them, and increasing your potential. You are taking control of your problems, accepting your flaws, and working through them so they no longer affect you. By doing this, you become more self-aware, and you remove the problems from your life that often manifest as belief barriers. Therefore, you raise your potential for greatness, and most importantly you remove the obstacles in your way.

CHAPTER 1: THE PROBLEM WITH POTENTIAL

PROBLEMS HAVE THE POTENTIAL TO GROW

Problems have the potential to grow. The problems I am talking about aren't physical, as some physical problems are out of your control like birth-related illnesses or defects; lots of other physical problems can be faced and prevented, but the main problems with potential I am talking about are mental. They are ethereal. They are real in that they exist within our minds, but they are also made up in our minds. These problems with potential are called belief barriers. Belief barriers are real and unreal at the same time because they are beliefs that are untrue about your true potential, but they are overwhelmingly convincing in your head due to the untrue assumption that your past mistakes dictate your future success.

Problems with potential all start as a mental battle in your mind. These problems are created in reality when you lose the battle of the mind. When your internal dialogue goes from discussing whether you should do the right thing or make the healthy choice to deciding that you don't need to do that right now (procrastination), problems arise.

Take physical fitness as an example. If you don't feel motivated to go to the gym, lack the willpower to eat healthy, or never make time for de-stressing, your physical health will decline. Your health will decline not because you are incapable of taking care of yourself, but because you haven't trained your mind to prioritize healthy activities. Even if you logically under-

THE PROBLEM WITH POTENTIAL

stand that not exercising your body you will have irreparable health consequences for the rest of your life, logic doesn't always demand action. Logic often leads to apathy. You know you should do the right thing, but you don't decide to do the right thing. This is due to your problems manifesting as emotional blocks that convince your mind they are impossible to overcome, so why try? The truth is that although starting to exercise and take care of yourself is difficult, it isn't impossible. If you face this specific problem in your mind known as motivation and decide to start exercising, your body will slowly but surely begin to repair itself! If you don't face your mental problem of procrastination, you will never do the things you dream of doing because you will always put your dreams off until tomorrow. And how you do one thing, such as the example of exercise, is often how you do everything. Life's choices are often made up of habitual decisions led by your problems or desire to achieve your potential.

Here's another example. You struggle with being empathetic, and you are a very logical-thinking person, like myself. If you never confront your lack of empathy, a habitual way of thinking, you will never truly have close long-term relationships because they require you to be vulnerable and empathetic to grow close to others.

If you never face your problems, they become worse, and worse and worse, and then... you stop trying because you've put a limit on yourself. You put your potential in a "box" that

CHAPTER 1: THE PROBLEM WITH POTENTIAL

is constricted by the fact that you don't think that you can overcome your problems. This box is all in your mind, created by long-term habitual thought patterns. These patterns can be changed if you are willing. The inspiration to change starts with understanding how valuable you are in this world. Once you figure out how important you and the decisions you make in the world are, you will begin to realize there is a purpose for your life. There is something that you've always wanted to do, but you didn't have the confidence to go after it just yet. But you will. Once you've discovered your purpose, all you have to do is start taking small steps in the direction of your purpose.

What is your purpose? To discover your purpose, you need to look deeper within yourself than you normally do. Your purpose is often misconstrued as passion, but passion is an emotion that will eventually fade. Your purpose is something you are willing to give up your life for. It's the reason you do anything. It's the bedrock of why you do what you do, and it's the most motivating force you'll ever experience once you've found what your purpose is in life.

Later in this book, I have written a chapter solely to inspire you to find and articulate your personal purpose. I've specifically chosen to put it towards the end of the book because finding your purpose isn't an overnight phenomenon. It takes a lot of thought, reflection, and belief in what is possible to open your mind to the possibilities of the impact you can have in this world. Therefore, I want to help you open your mind before the in-depth look at starting to find your purpose in life. Sometimes finding purpose is difficult if you struggle to build good habits and procrastinate.

FACING YOUR PROBLEMS BUILDS CONFIDENCE

Even if you don't know your purpose yet, facing your problems will open your mind to possibilities for your life that you didn't expect—just by building your confidence in what you believe you can accomplish. You can and will change these patterns by taking the first step in overcoming your problems, even if you don't *believe* you can overcome them... <u>*yet*</u>. Even if you don't believe you are worthy or skilled enough to reach your potential and achieve extraordinary results in life, you will start believing that you can after you've taken enough steps in the right direction to prove to yourself that you will eventually get there. The first step is the hardest. It's like deciding to run a marathon when you haven't run in several years. Running the marathon seems impossible, but if you start training and continue to take steps over weeks and months leading up to the race, you will feel more prepared. The race will be less daunting. The length or difficulty of the race hasn't changed, but you have changed. You have become stronger. You have developed a belief in yourself that you can conquer the race. It all started with taking the frightful first step months earlier when you still

CHAPTER 1: THE PROBLEM WITH POTENTIAL

didn't believe that you could even complete the race. So, write down one habit holding you back right now that you know you need to change and schedule time in your week to tackle this problem. If you are disorganized, then schedule an hour to get more organized. If you are late, be early this week. If you are angry, start doing yoga. If you are lonely, join a networking club. If you are addicted to your phone, read a book and put your phone down for an hour. Get started, no excuses.

Imagine every person on the planet was like an electrical circuit connected to a light switch. If you click the switch on, electricity flows and from this tiny little switch, you can turn on a light that *lights up the room.* Electricity flows faster than you could ever imagine the moment the switch is flipped, and beautiful light is created for the ENTIRE room to enjoy! Everyone benefits from the light generated by turning on the light. The potential is always there to light up the room, but it all comes down to the switch being turned on. In this case, you are the only person who can flip the switch.

The switch represents your ability to make decisions. The light (or the absence of light) represents how you influence the people around you in the room. If you flip the switch "on" and turn your mind on to the possibilities of how much potential you have, people will not only see you become more intentional in your life, but they will also be inspired by you. Confronting your problems isn't just about you. It's also about inspiring those around you to do the same.

THE PROBLEM WITH POTENTIAL

The problem with potential is that *potential* is all in your head. It's not real. It's nothing. It's just potential. It's what could happen if all the *right* things fell into place. It's what could happen when everything else happens first. It's what would happen if you *actually* gave it your all. It's a "what-if?" Unfortunately, what-if isn't helping you, and it isn't helping anyone else either. What-if is the question you ask when your internal thought dialogue is trying to convince you about how you will fail or how you should *procrastinate*.

WHAT IF?

What if something bad happens? What if I fail? What if I don't hit my goals or reach my potential? Welcome to the most common and decisive internal dialogue that you will continually have your entire life. This what-if conversation is on replay in everyone's mind. It represents how the human mind is wired to avoid pain. The what-if dialogue creates immense fearful responses that reach your entire body through cortisol rushing through your veins as you imagine the worst-case scenario. Everyone has a similar but different internal dialogue based on their past experiences, failures, and successes. We all have a version of the what-if conversation. Some of these conversations are more intense than others, but even if there are varying degrees to this conversation based on varying circumstances, you still have the ability to *decide* how you will react to your circumstances

CHAPTER 1: THE PROBLEM WITH POTENTIAL

and internal dialogues. The dialogue doesn't control you, you control the dialogue, but you may not understand that the internal dialogue is based on your habitual thinking patterns processed in your subconscious. Everyone has developed habits, good and bad, and every person has some sort of internal dialogue going on in their minds. Everyone has different strengths and weaknesses, and therefore different potential and different outcomes in life. The critical takeaway is that reaching *your unique* potential is less about the fact that internal dialogue and differentiating external circumstances exist, and more about how you *react* to the dialogue and your circumstances. Long-term extraordinary achievement is based on how you allow this internal dialogue to affect you, and how you learn to control it. Isn't that an encouraging thought? You are in charge of how things affect you, no one else.

To control your emotions, you need to examine your self-talk. Self-talk is your internal dialogue of what you say to yourself about yourself and what you believe about what others say about you. Unfortunately, self-talk often correlates with comparing yourself to others. I call this the comparison trap. The comparison trap is the idea that you avoid doing things or make yourself feel incapable of comparison to the perceived abilities of others. Your happiness and success should not be dependent on the comparison between you and others as every person is unique with unique talents, goals, and aspirations. In Don Clifton's book, *Strengths-Based Leadership*, Clifton and his team interviewed over 20,000 leaders in 1960. They conducted nearly identical ninety-minute experiments across as many industries as possible. They even looked at public performance data to cross-reference with the type of answers they received from their leadership questions so they could evaluate the data as objectively as possible. Clifton concluded that there is no definitive, objective list of leadership qualities that describes all great leaders. The leadership qualities themselves are less important. What is more valuable is how a leader knows their strengths and utilities them at the right times: "As a carpenter knows his tools or a physician knows the instrument at her disposal, what great leaders have in common is that each truly knows his or her strengths—and can call on the right strength at the right time."[5] Therefore, you ought to accept yourself for who you are. What your strengths and weaknesses are matter less than knowing your strengths and learning when to use them. You first must believe in yourself by not comparing yourself to others and developing healthy self-talk.

What you believe about what others say about you is a choice. You choose what you believe or do not believe. You have control over your internal dialogue. It is also a choice. Choices become habitual. If you consistently believe what everyone says about you, you might feel you aren't in control of those choices because habits are stored in your subconscious. If you are consistently negative to yourself and you habitually tell yourself you can't do things, you will eventually

---

[5] Rath, T. & Conchie, B. (2017). *Strengths Based Leadership: Great Leaders, Teams, and Why People Follow*. Gallup Press.

CHAPTER 1: THE PROBLEM WITH POTENTIAL

believe your statements—even if they aren't true—because they have become habits and thus, are a part of your subconscious. Taking control of yourself means that you begin to actively monitor and intentionally work to make your internal dialogue more encouraging and filter out the lies of what people say about you. This can be done by simply journaling each night before or by speaking positive and encouraging phrases out loud when you feel the urge to think negatively. As you start to filter out comparisons with others instead of internalizing what they say, you can start developing a more positive mindset and outlook on life. You can begin to see that success in any career or part of life starts at step one.

Success is not by accident; there is always a backstory to success and accomplishments. Once you realize that everyone you "idolize" started out as normal people just like you, you can instead look at their journey and then *replicate* it, or better yet, *invent a new story*. The only difference between you and them is they got excited about an idea and decided to be disciplined enough to master their internal dialogue in such a way that the "what-ifs" didn't stop them. Then they solved their problems through consistent action rather than procrastinating. They started taking realistic steps towards reaching their potential because they developed personal beliefs in themselves after overcoming the problems they *thought* were too big to overcome. They thought their problems were stronger than them, but they weren't. Remember, limits come from allowing your internal dialogue to define you, rather than defining how you will react to it.

Notice that to achieve great things, you can't skip over your problems and expect to reach your absolute highest potential. What you must do is unshackle yourself from the "box" you put yourself in by taking small steps towards training your mind and your body to face your problems in real life.

The small steps have to do with your integrity. *Integrity is what you do when no one is looking.* When no one is looking, you reveal your true colors. Developing the art of discipline takes time and failure, but you can develop the habit of always doing what you say you will do, even if no one checks in on you; your problems will start to melt away due to your consistent effort to face them. The easiest and most accessible way to do this is through writing down your goals for your life, developing a personal schedule for your week that mirrors your goals, and committing to doing hard things within that schedule to develop confidence anchors, or personal belief, like exercising, reading, and challenging yourself to develop discipline and the mental toughness needed for long-term consistency.

WHY HAVING GOALS MATTERS

In 2015, a study by the Dominican University of California[6] found that goals make a massive difference in your success. They took 149 participants and put them into five separate groups

---

6 Gardner, Sarah and Albee, Dave, *Study focuses on strategies for achieving goals, resolutions* (2015). Press Releases. 266.
https://scholar.dominican.edu/news-releases/266

CHAPTER 1: THE PROBLEM WITH POTENTIAL

with different goal-setting strategies. In group one, they had participants "simply think about goals they hoped to accomplish in a four-week block," along with a ranking exercise to see how realistic the goals were to achieve based on their resources.
In groups two through five, they had participants do the same exercise as group one but also write their goals down. In group three, they had participants go even further and write "action commitments for each goal." Group four went even further and added an extraordinary step by sharing their goals with a friend. In group five, they went the furthest by doing everything previously stated, plus sending a weekly progress report to a friend. What they found is staggering.

Group one had 43% of participants either "accomplish their goals or be more than halfway there." Group two saw a success rate of 61%, while group four saw a 64% success rate. Impressively, group five saw a 76% success rate in its participants reaching their goals!

As you might have guessed, just by having goals, you are more likely to achieve them than by not having them. And, of course, if you write something versus just trying to remember it, you are more likely to achieve that goal. It's why to-do lists work better than "to-do thoughts." We often forget our own thoughts. And if you make actionable steps and break down your goals, they are even easier to achieve, especially when you commit to a friend. And, if you're regularly tracking your progress and sending it to a friend, you are more motivated to achieve that goal and don't want to let your friend down. So, to achieve great things, start replicating group five's goalsetting processes.

GOALS
1.
2.
3.
4.
5.
6.
7.

Figure 1.1: A simple list of your goals will help you organize your dreams in one place. There is a fillable goals sheet in the *Problem With Potential Workbook* you can use to organize your most important goals.

Since I heard of this study and even beforehand, I have written specific goals for every year of my life. I've written action plans. I've even shared them with friends and kept track of my progress. I have life goals, yearly goals, monthly goals, weekly goals, daily goals, and even goals for what to accomplish every thirty minutes for every hour of every day. To build your goals into your life, you must first create your goals without worrying about how possible they are, and then you must implement your goals into your daily and weekly lifestyle, tell a trusted friend, and track your progress with them if you want to achieve your goals in life. Building this network of personal accountability will keep you focused on taking action toward reaching your true potential. Since I heard of this study and even beforehand, I have written specific goals for every year. I have life goals, yearly goals, monthly goals, weekly goals, daily goals, and even goals for what to accomplish every thirty

CHAPTER 1: THE PROBLEM WITH POTENTIAL

minutes for every hour of the week. To build your goals into your life, you must first create your goals without worrying about how possible they are, and then you must implement your goals into your daily and weekly lifestyle.

WHAT ARE GOALS?

What are goals, and how do you come up with *your* goals? A goal is an achievement or vision of the future you desire to make a reality. Often goals are misnamed as dreams. Many people's dreams are their goals. They just call them dreams because they don't believe in themselves enough to believe that they are even possible, *yet*. Regardless of whether you think of your dreams as goals or your goals as dreams, write down fifty of your life goals on a sheet of paper. Whatever they are, don't overthink it and dare to dream. Now categorize your fifty life goals into the following areas: spiritual, family, professional, financial, social, health and fitness, giving, and personal growth and development. Faith-based or religious goals go into the spiritual category. Family and relationship goals go into the family category. Career and income-related goals go into the professional category. Financial and retirement goals go into the financial category. Friendship and lifestyle goals go into the social category. Fitness and physical health goals go into the health and fitness category. Philanthropy and donations goals go into the giving category. Finally, education and growth goals go into the personal growth and development category. Categorizing your goals can help you compartmentalize them into different parts of your day.

THE PROBLEM WITH POTENTIAL

Once categorized, reflect and add any other goals you may have forgotten. Clear written goals are only half the battle. The other half is beginning to take steps toward them. To do this, you must not look at the end result of each goal or you will become overwhelmed. You need to look at the process and work backward from the end results, step by step, until you get to where you currently are with achieving that goal. This is called *crystallizing* your goals. You must crystalize, or break down, your big goals into very small goals. The best analogy I have heard for this is to imagine you are tasked with eating an elephant. Could you do it? The mind often jumps to the conclusion that there is no way that you could eat an elephant. This is because the mind often thinks of instant gratification. Meaning that your mind thinks that you have to eat the whole elephant *today*. But the reality is there is no such stipulation with the question. Can you eat an elephant? The answer is yes. By eating a small piece of elephant meat every day, you can eat a whole elephant. Breaking down your goal into small bite-sized chunks (pun intended) allows your mind to *believe* that you can accomplish the greater goal. If you instead look at the whole elephant, you will be overwhelmed and believe that you cannot do it, therefore you will procrastinate ever starting. So, if you want to learn how to lead people, start practicing leading yourself first, then small groups, then larger groups, and so on. You don't magically become a fantastic leader just because you have the goal and desire to lead; you do so through small steps of improvement through experience, research, and consistency.

CHAPTER 1: THE PROBLEM WITH POTENTIAL

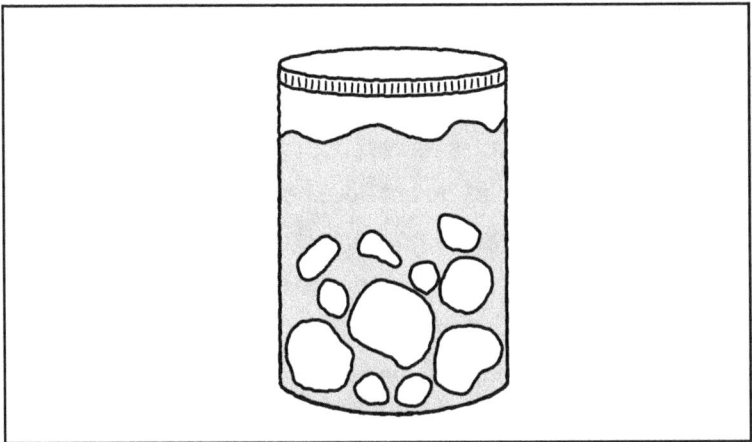

Figure 1.2: **The jar represents your time. The rocks represent your priorities. The pebbles represent important activities that are flexible. Surrounding the rocks and pebbles is sand, your least important activities.**

When developing a personal schedule, your schedule should mirror your goals. You have limited time and must use it wisely to reach your potential. To organize, Imagine you have a jar filled with air in front of you. The jar represents a week's worth of time because there is a limit of twenty-four hours a day, resulting in 168 hours a week. There is a limit to the amount of time you have access to the jar. Time is scarce. Therefore, you must manage your limited time because you can never get back even one second. Therefore, time is the greatest asset.

ROCKS, PEBBLES, SAND

I once heard an incredible strategy at a conference that I now use daily to organize my time and utilize when I coach my business clients: filling your jar with rocks, pebbles, and sand. These objects represent activities you spend

THE PROBLEM WITH POTENTIAL

your time on. The rocks represent your goals. They are the most important and valuable things you can spend time on. Rocks are priorities. The rocks have negative repercussions if neglected. The pebbles represent things that are valuable but are flexible. Pebbles do not have negative repercussions if neglected. Sand is free time. Sand is unimportant and can be moved anywhere. If you never used sand, nothing terrible would happen. Each category of object is subjective to a point and objective to a point. For example, sleep is ALWAYS a rock because without sleep you will hallucinate, function at a lower cognitive level, and eventually die without it. Practicing the guitar could be a rock to some *or* a pebble to others. If you are in the band Aerosmith, practicing the guitar is your way of life and one of your goals and things you are passionate about, then spending time perfecting your craft is of utmost importance to you. If you neglect to practice the guitar and begin to perform poorly, your fans might leave and cause your source of income to cease, causing negative repercussions. You might become depressed that you are failing at your goal of being a rock star. If you are practicing the guitar as a hobby in your free time, then if you miss a day or take a month off, your way of life isn't negatively affected other than you miss out on the enjoyment of your hobby. In both cases, sleep is still a rock. A rock can be rest if you are someone who works themselves into chronic stress. Rest can be sand if you struggle with disciplining yourself to work. Eating food to sustain your body is always a rock. Eating healthy should always be a rock but is often a pebble or sand. You decide what your rocks, pebbles, and sand are based on the goals you have for your life.

CHAPTER 1: THE PROBLEM WITH POTENTIAL

	M	T	W	Th	F
9:00					
10:00					
11:00					
12:00					
1:00					
2:00					
3:00					
4:00					
5:00					
6:00					
7:00					
8:00					
9:00					

Figure 1.3: This is a simple schedule that you can use to organize your time by hour. There is a fillable schedule in the *Problem With Potential Workbook* you can use to organize your weekly routine.

Now imagine fitting the objects into the jar. If you put sand, then pebbles, then rocks, you won't be able to fit in the most possible rocks. If you put anything other than rocks first, you will be limited in the number of rocks you can put into your week. Your rocks, pebbles, and sand must be aligned with your goals and purpose for your life to reach your potential. How you spend your time in your week should reflect your overall goals in life. Then you prioritize how you fit them into your week to reach your goals.

YOUR GOAL SHOULD REFLECT YOUR SCHEDULE

If you have the goal of becoming a business leader, there should be a time in your weekly schedule when you are becoming a better businessperson and a better leader; if not, then you are procrastinating your goals. If you look at your week's schedule and your goals, they should be synonymous. You should see steps being taken to reach your goals each week. If you don't see this, your weekly schedule doesn't reflect your goals and must be reworked and reworked until your time is partitioned in the right manner.

In my experience, the best way to start your day is with your most difficult and creative tasks. These tasks often require the most energy, and you can accomplish them much more easily with a fresh and undistracted mind that allows you to focus on tackling the tasks. I intentionally place my easiest tasks in the afternoon, because by the end of the day, I have become fatigued and am looking forward to relaxing, socializing, or exercising. I know that I can still get the easy things done even if I am fatigued. In general, the weekends are when I put my rocks to rest with a lot of my sand and pebbles, as there is less urgency to perform at a high level professionally due to the time off of everyone else. This seems the best time to ensure you rest. Rest is an unconditional rock, as you can only work so hard for so long before you begin to resent your schedule. For example, human beings experience immense negative effects when they become isolated, so you physically and mentally

CHAPTER 1: THE PROBLEM WITH POTENTIAL

will perform worse if you don't rest, relax, and spend time with loved ones and friends.

Reaching your goals in life, even with an incredibly specific personal schedule that mirrors your goals, still requires a great deal of mental toughness, discipline, and consistency. Even if you plan and write everything out to perfection, you must still take action. You must develop the habit of taking action even when you don't want to because reaching your goals requires you to grow. This is why I love starting the day with physical fitness. If you start the day doing sprints, squats, or any sort of workout, it requires you to do something uncomfortable when you often least want to do it. When you push yourself in the morning and make that conscious decision to get out of bed and grow your muscles, you are developing the mental habits you need to continue through the day and follow through on your schedule. When you start your day with the most difficult thing, everything else looks easy. You begin to look at the rest of your challenges and compare them to those that you just ran several miles or worked out hard for an hour. Then you carry your momentum from a massive victory in the morning to each task on your schedule and you accomplish as much as you can day after day. As you consistently take steps towards reaching your goals, your mind will start to *believe* that you are capable of doing anything you put your mind to, and it will begin to turn these past successes into confidence anchors.

Confidence anchors are moments in your life that you can look back on with *confidence* and know that because you

THE PROBLEM WITH POTENTIAL

have accomplished this difficult thing, you can accomplish the next! A great example is after you've run a half-marathon, you will feel much more confident in doing it again or taking on a greater running challenge, like a full marathon. Confidence anchors drive the rest of what you do in your life. If you can create confidence anchors, you will be more and more excited to take on new and bigger challenges. That's why you should start your day with challenges, as that practice creates a daily confidence anchor that you can look back on for the rest of the day. When you implement these habits —even for just a year's time—you will be able to look back at how you started a year later, and not only will you be more physically fit and confident than you were when you started, but you will also see just how far you have come in a short period of time. Developing a larger confidence anchor that will propel you even further than the small daily wins of your schedule.

In the next few chapters, you are going to walk through some of the hardest things you will have to conquer to overcome procrastination and begin firing on all cylinders and reaching your potential. Once you start overcoming your problems, you will begin to unlock your true potential and, most importantly, you will begin to REALIZE that potential by taking steps towards achieving incredible things! From you doing this, others will be influenced by it and hopefully do the same.

Confront your problems and unlock your mindset and potential. Most of all, don't let your past dictate your future.

CHAPTER 2

WHY THE WORLD NEEDS YOU TO REACH YOUR POTENTIAL

The world needs your skills, talents, and passions more than you could imagine!
Never forget how important you are to helping others.

I remember when I was nineteen, I took an opportunity to go on a mission trip. We were going to Nicaragua with one of my mentors from my summer internship at the time and nine other students from the Southwestern internship I had been doing the past two summers. The mission trip was my first one out of the country, and I was so excited for the experience. I wanted to grow close to God, and I desperately wanted to see new parts of the world and help people. The trip was pretty costly at the time, but I did feel better knowing that most of the money would be going towards the mission we were going to support called One Collective.

At the time, I was going to the University of Tennessee, studying accounting and finance, and my flight to Nicaragua was flying out of the Atlanta International Airport. I was on the same flight as my mentor at the time, Trey, his daughter, and another student whom I hadn't met before, named Walton.

At that time, I was pretty good at procrastinating. In fact, I still didn't study very much before tests or read the textbooks for ANY of my classes. I did show up though, which was a good habit. But you see, because of these bad habits of waiting until the last minute, I failed to plan properly for my three-hour drive to Atlanta. For those of you who have never flown out of the Atlanta airport, it is probably one of the busiest airports in the world.

I was leaving school right after one of my classes. (Life tip: always pack the night before a trip, so you aren't late to the airport and miss a flight.) I started the journey south, and I planned to get to the airport about an hour and a half early. I thought that would be enough wiggle room. Generally, for an international flight, you should arrive about two hours early to ensure you get everything processed correctly with plenty of time to spare. In my case, I didn't know any better and was trying to make it work just like getting to class three minutes early.

CHAPTER 2: WHY THE WORLD NEEDS YOU TO REACH YOUR POTENTIAL

I was driving somewhere in northern Georgia, and then… I got stuck in standstill traffic. I knew I was going to be late, and the panic started.

Fast-forward to arriving in Atlanta, I got to the parking area with about forty-five minutes until my flight was to take off. This is not an appropriate arrival time. I got out of my car and sprinted to the shuttle. I got to the actual airport about thirty minutes from takeoff. I wasn't even through security, let alone in line, on a busy Friday evening. I was going to miss my flight.

I remember jogging as fast as I could with my luggage and then… you guessed it, another wonder of the world: lots and lots of people standing in a very packed line. My heart sank. I was going to miss my flight, and there wouldn't be another flight until the next day. I did what any rational person would do; I accepted defeat and prayed for a miracle.

As I was walking, a flight attendant let someone cut in front of the line because they were in a wheelchair. I told her I was about to miss my flight to a mission trip, and for some reason… she offered to let me cut in front of about 500 people out of nowhere… It was one of the most bizarre things I had ever experienced. There were hundreds of people waiting in line. With no injuries and no wheelchair, she let me go right on through the line. I ended up sprinting to the doors as my group was boarding. The last passengers waiting on me bought me time and held the doors open. I couldn't believe I made it.

THE PROBLEM WITH POTENTIAL

Do you believe in miracles? I believe that God made a miracle happen that day. I don't know for sure, but I do know that for some weird reason, I was allowed to reach the flight when I shouldn't have. No one else got special treatment at that moment, and I normally don't get special treatment either. I don't think I'm overly special, but rather I think that God has these small moments in store for our lives when we often least expect it. Catching that flight made a massive difference in my life, and the experience helped shape me into who I am today.

I have always been thankful for that moment. Because on that trip, my perspective on life completely changed. Although I still struggle with negativity and frustration in my life, I was being molded to think differently and see the world through a different lens. I knew that God wanted me to start focusing on becoming a light for others in my life journey. The first step was teaching me that money doesn't bring happiness, and neither do worldly possessions, but rather helping others.

After an eight-hour flight, I arrived with my group at the Nicaraguan airport. We were absolutely exhausted after experiencing a flight on a cheap airline with metal seats without the ability to recline. Groggy, we all hustled into a van at 2:00 a.m. We were in and out of sleep for a bumpy two-hour van drive to a little city called Masatepe. Masatepe was around 40,000 Nicaraguans with very few cars. The cars they did have were old and beaten up from the previous millennia.

CHAPTER 2: WHY THE WORLD NEEDS YOU TO REACH YOUR POTENTIAL

I remember getting dropped off from the van and settling into the modest quarters where about six men shared a living space for the next ten days. There was no air conditioning, and there was just one rickety ceiling fan that continuously swirled, looking as if it might fall down at any moment. Regardless of the new and contrasting environment to what I was used to, I fell asleep the second my head hit the pillow.

I woke up the next day to an incredible breakfast of rice and beans with all of these tasty Nicaraguan dishes like breakfast quesadillas and this interesting juice that I don't remember the name of. The very first meeting was with the leader of the organization in Masatepe from the missionary organization, One Collective. We listened to him intently as he was very authentic and genuine, and I believe he had been living in the community away from all of the luxuries of America for more than five years. He knew what he was doing. In fact, he introduced a life-changing concept to me called the Ovarian Lottery.

THE OVARIAN LOTTERY

Oftentimes we need metaphors to really understand impactful concepts; that is what the Ovarian Lottery is. It is a metaphor that will help you understand the world from a more holistic perspective. Here's the explanation of what the Ovarian Lottery is.

THE PROBLEM WITH POTENTIAL

Imagine a lottery with eight billion numbers, and let's say that everyone gets something from the lottery. The last-place ticket could be being born blind or with a disability or a disease that you had no control over. One of the lowest tickets aside from a physical or mental disability would be like being born into a Dalit, or untouchable, family in India outside the standard Hindu caste system. In that society, Dalits are believed by the Hindu religion to be reincarnated beings who were evil and had terrible karma in their past lives. Karma is the sum of their good deeds compared to their evil deeds. Dalits are believed to have had such bad karma that they are being punished in the present by being scorned and ridiculed in this life. According to National Geographic,[7] there was a "Dalit boy beaten to death for plucking flowers and a Dalit tortured by the cops for three days," among other atrocities. The Dalits have no control over who they are and what they were born to, but they are treated this way from birth to death. To really understand what it is like to be untouchable, imagine being born and everyone thinking you are worthless because of something you never personally did. They won't touch you because they don't want you to rub off on them.

On the other hand, the first-place ticket is being born as a child of Bill Gates, one of the wealthiest people of all time. His children have every opportunity in life and access to many incredible connections, businesses, and wealth that their dad worked hard to build over his life. Knowing you are

---

[7] Mayell, H. (2021, May 4). *India's "Untouchables" face violence, discrimination.* Pages. https://www.nationalgeographic.com/pages/article/indias-untouchables-face-violence-discrimination

CHAPTER 2: WHY THE WORLD NEEDS YOU TO REACH YOUR POTENTIAL

a Gates commands respect from your peers, businesses, donors, and politicians. And, of course, there is every lottery ticket between the Dalit and being born to the wealthiest man on the planet. Somewhere, your lottery ticket exists.

There is a 17% chance of being born in a developed country with access to healthcare, good infrastructure, and a sound education system. There is an 83% chance that you will be born somewhere without consistent access to these basic necessities. Nine out of every ten under-five-year-old deaths happen in a developing country.[1] No matter what your situation is, you are lucky to be alive. If you're reading this and live in a developed country, you are blessed with an education, a family of some sort, money to buy this book, and the opportunity to pursue a multitude of career options. You have freedoms many countries don't offer their citizens, and you have so much to be thankful for.

Some tickets are better than others. Some are worse. No matter what ticket you win, it wasn't your choice. Although you don't get to choose your lottery ticket, and you can't change who you were born to or how you grew up, there is something you can choose: how you react to it. Life is 10% what happens to you and 90% how you react to it.

Globally, 2.4-billion people lack access to improved sanitation, including nearly 950 million who are forced to resort to open defecation for lack of other options.[8]

---

[8] *Lack of Sanitation for 2.4 Billion People is Undermining Health Improvements*. (2015, June 30). World Health Organization. https://tinyurl.com/lackofsanitation

THE PROBLEM WITH POTENTIAL

This might not be something you've ever worried about. Still, nearly one in three births worldwide are never officially recorded, depriving those children of their right to name, public services essential for survival, and nationality.

Globally, nearly one in five children under five aren't immunized today. That's a real problem, but one we can solve: infant and childhood vaccinations save an estimated two to three million lives every year. The missionary told us that we should be eternally thankful that we were blessed to be where we are today financially based on sheer probability.

I chewed on this idea for the rest of the week as I was trying to see the world in a new light. Throughout that week, I saw a lot of things that reinforced this idea of the Ovarian Lottery. I saw propaganda trucks every night blasting authoritarian dogma in the streets. I had heard about things like this, but experiencing one was totally different. I saw old beat-up cars from the 90s that were few and far between. But if you had one, it meant you were wealthy. I thought I had it rough sharing a truck with my two older brothers growing up while my parents had two other vehicles. I played soccer in a field of rocks and sand with very little grass with some of the teenagers. I met some of the most joyful and caring people I had ever seen. I saw families finding ways to have fun and spend time together, and I saw churches full of believers. I heard about witch-towns just a couple hours' drive away, and I saw missionaries teaching the local population how to

CHAPTER 2: WHY THE WORLD NEEDS YOU TO REACH YOUR POTENTIAL

create businesses and thrive through skills and education. I got to weed whack the old-fashioned way for eight hours with a machete, and I had some of the best food I'd ever tasted. The lack of wealth and money didn't make these people unhappy, but rather it helped them to work together. Regardless of their financial status, people enjoyed life as best they could and made do with what they had.

What I didn't see was a lot of people watching TV, complaining about what they didn't have, and people unhappy that they *had to go to class in college* or attend another boring business seminar. People weren't complaining about going to doctors' appointments or the dentist. And I was reminded about how I had done this before and how lucky I was even to have the chance to attend school, attend a business seminar, or go to a regular doctor or dentist. I used to decide to be unhappy based on how entertained I was mentally rather than based on being thankful for the life I did have.

I saw people trying to find joy in every moment because they didn't have very much more than each other. This trip changed my life by showing me more of the world than my little bubble back home. In this bubble was a world of people who: weren't happy with their jobs; always needed to get the next, more expensive phone or car; and measured their value based on comparisons to others' statuses. And I had done the same up until that moment. Was my true potential really to gain a bunch

THE PROBLEM WITH POTENTIAL

of stuff but be perpetually unhappy because someone always had more than me? Was there a better way to live life and truly make a difference that wasn't just for my personal gain?

The trip ended after ten days and countless stories. The ONE THING I can't stop thinking about, to this day, is the idea of the Ovarian Lottery. This one concept completely changed my perspective on life because before learning it, I used just to do things for myself and my happiness, but I realized wholeheartedly how selfish it was to have such average goals in life. Average goals of making money and living comfortably. I used to desperately want to "be happy and like my job," but now I navigate through life knowing there is so much more to life than trying to be happy, and that is helping others.

Now that you know what the Ovarian Lottery is, what do you do with it? We are now confronted with the following questions: What am I doing with what I've won from the Ovarian Lottery? What is the one thing I can do that no one else can do? How can I add value to the people around me? What kind of life do I want to lead?

Winning the Ovarian Lottery puts you in a small percentage of people who have access to knowledge that many don't—meaning that, on average, you have a greater propensity to really change the world. What is incredible is that plenty of people **lost** the Ovarian Lottery and still have made a global difference. Your potential has nothing to do with the cards you are dealt, but rather with what you do with them. So, you

CHAPTER 2: WHY THE WORLD NEEDS YOU TO REACH YOUR POTENTIAL

shouldn't be frightened. If others can do it, so can you. The world needs you. People need you to reach your potential. For so few people truly strive for their best in life. I don't know you—or your strengths and weaknesses—but maybe your job is to simply share what you know, maybe it's to invent something, maybe it's to start a business or a nonprofit, or to become an author of ideas worth sharing. Maybe you are just supposed to be the person who shows up when no one else does. Maybe you're supposed to be a teacher, a doctor, or a lawyer. With whatever skills, talents, and time you have, we all need you to reach your potential. When you reach your potential, you will be helping others in some way that you wouldn't be if you hadn't achieved the best results in life that you could. Whether you become the president or CEO of a massive company, or some other major position isn't important. What is important is that you find the problem that you can solve for others and seek to make the world a better place. The only way to do this is by becoming the best version of yourself in the pursuit of helping others. For your mind is limited by your growth and so is your ability to achieve great things and help others.

DON'T FOCUS ON MATERIALISM

Reaching your potential isn't just about being incredibly successful in the sense of materialism, but instead based on your impact on the world. Materialism is the worship of money and possessions. Suppose you become materialistically wealthy at the expense of others. In that case, you are not becoming the best version of yourself or reaching your potential because you are not adding as much as you possibly could to benefit of others. Your ultimate ability to make money or become wealthy is less important than how you spend it and where your heart lies. If you become a billionaire but are lonely, selfish, and egotistical, you've missed the entire point of why becoming successful is even valuable. In Simon Sinek's book *The Infinite Game*, he talks about how every infinitely minded business requires a just cause or will eventually fail. A just cause is the purpose behind why the business exists. For example, at my company, our mission is to inspire people to bridge their knowledge gaps, think big, and believe in themselves so that they can do what inspires them and add value to the people around them and, together, we can make the world a better place. The money I make is fuel to further this just cause of helping others work together to make the world a better place. A just cause or purpose for your life works the same as it does for a business. You must have direction. Without a personal cause or purpose, success becomes all about us. Money becomes an addiction and materialistic things become the focus. The question becomes, "How do I improve my situation?" rather than, "How do I use my talents to help make the world a better place?"

When you succeed with what you've been gifted, you will reach and impact more people. To do that, you must face

CHAPTER 2: WHY THE WORLD NEEDS YOU TO REACH YOUR POTENTIAL

your problems with potential. In doing so, you will unlock the pathway to reaching your best results and the best version of yourself. What you end up achieving will be bigger and more life-changing than you realize. Regardless of the outcome, just by partaking in the process of intentionally trying to become the best version of yourself and reach your potential to achieve big things, you will—at the very least—inspire those around you to do the same.

The real question is, why doesn't everyone do just that?

CHAPTER 3

THE FALLACY OF PROFICIENCY

Who decides if you like something?

After college, I was a full-time recruiter for four years for the Southwestern Company, the same company I worked at as an undergraduate. From the ages of twenty-one to twenty-five, I led a cohort of students on one of the most challenging summer internships you could do. The program helped college students make money, gain experience, and—most importantly—challenge themselves. In fact, on its face, the program looked so challenging that a massive percentage of people judged it as impossible. I worked at that company for seven years, and it was one of the best decisions I ever made in my young adult years because it challenged me to act and

THE PROBLEM WITH POTENTIAL

make things happen—and it taught me how to think positively. It was such a challenging experience that you had to develop your mental toughness and look at the glass half full, or you would get crushed and quit. I was fortunate to have enough support from my family, friends, and program leaders to do the former; my life is entirely different because of it.

As I was recruiting students to sell in our program, I typically had a team of around ten or so each year. I was also personally responsible for training each student. Their success was nearly wholly dependent upon my training. I loved teaching students how to control their mindset in those training sessions. I would recruit students with big goals in life, and with big goals come many steps.

Often, I had bright-minded and enthusiastic young people working with me, and my job would be helping them develop the necessary skills to reach their life goals. Some students I worked with wanted to be lawyers, business owners, investment bankers, etc. I rarely worked with a student who didn't have significant goals. These students learned that reaching these challenging career goals took a lot of effort. By selling door-to-door, they would become master communicators, masters of their minds, and develop an unparalleled work ethic. Not to mention, they would often be able to pay for their college tuition from the money they made and graduate debt-free. These students would even become part of a lifelong network of over 100,000 successful alums, many of

CHAPTER 3: THE FALLACY OF PROFICIENCY

whom were in their fields and looked for talent who did the Southwestern program. Still, these talented students often talked themselves out of giving the internship their all or found "reasons" why they should procrastinate preparation.

For most of these students, there was no quicker way to gain as many life skills, communication skills, and alumni connections than by going all out and proving themselves in the internship. But to do that, it would require a herculean effort. To inspire these students to reach their long-term goals, I was tasked with helping them get excited about the short-term challenges.

There were always moments in training when a talented student would avoid memorizing their sales talk. When that happened, I would always ask them the following question—especially when they decided to complain about the small stuff. "Who decides if you like something?" The student would stare at me dumbfounded for about ten seconds, and then they would look me right in the eye and say, "I decide if I like something." I would follow up with, "And how do you decide if you like something?" The student would usually get stuck here. "The lesson is that learning your sales talk [we would say a sales script to a client when selling] will ultimately be better for you this summer than not learning it. Correct? Therefore, learning it will improve your life and help you sell more. Thus proving yourself to your future employers that you are capable and more impressive than other applicants. Correct? So, the question is, why is it so difficult to get started? The reason is that you aren't good at it yet, and because you aren't good at your sales talk, the only way to become good at your sales talk is through practice and failure. If you connect learning your sales talk to your ultimate success, you can get excited about the challenging (and sometimes monotonous) task of memorizing a script."

The students wouldn't even know what to say or think, and after this conversation, my students would no longer complain. They began to take ownership of their likes and dislikes because they wanted to reach their potential in life. They realized that what they liked or disliked was completely based on their own mindset rather than the value of the task. If you can associate the short-term pain of learning a new skill with the long-term benefit, you can get excited about it and get started.

Because of these new mental habits, my students were able to look at challenges and find ways to like or enjoy what most people would see as difficult or frustrating. This simple mentality would allow many of them to go on and be in the top 2% of door-to-door salespeople in the world during the summer.

LOOK AT THE BIGGER PICTURE

This mentality transcends many different aspects of life, but in this case, I was challenging the students on why they didn't like to do something. Whether it's doing dishes or knocking on doors, there are benefits to the activity that you can get excited about if you look at the bigger picture rather than the

CHAPTER 3: THE FALLACY OF PROFICIENCY

short-term cost. As with washing the dishes or knocking on a door, they both are annoying at times. You might be doing something that isn't the top thing to do on your priority list or something that isn't your greatest strength, but doing that thing can still bring you joy, help you grow, and you can make it more fun. For example, when you wash the dishes, it takes time; but in the end, you feel a sense of cleanliness and accomplishment. Now, if you wash the dishes to your favorite song, you can make the experience more enjoyable. When knocking on doors, although it can be frustrating the number of nos you get, you are also developing endurance and discipline to keep going. Regardless of the result, you can take pride in the process of pushing yourself to get rejected in order to grow. There would even be times that I would bring a carrot to the door, knock, and take a bite when they walked out saying, "What's up doc?" like Bugs Bunny. I would almost always get a laugh and a smiling parent willing to talk to me for just a few minutes regardless of their interest in the products because I brought joy to their door. I only did this after I had knocked on countless doors beforehand to build up my confidence to be able to pull that off. Had I done that the first door I ever knocked on, I probably would have confused the homeowner to the point of frustration! But after countless hours of knocking, I could now make the job fun.

Taking ownership and deciding if you do or don't like something gives you the opportunity to reflect and examine your mental weaknesses and resolve to change them. This matters not because you should "force" yourself to enjoy mundane tasks, but rather, it will help you see difficult steps as exciting challenges to overcome rather than barriers to success. After all, as you improve, you will become better at the task. When you get better, you start to see results. As you see results, you start taking steps toward your goals and achieving the results you were looking for.

Not only can you see the bigger picture and get excited to do hard things because of the long-term benefits, but you can also manipulate your environment to make things more enjoyable with music, friends, or a carrot prop when knocking on doors. This is, by definition, how you grow.

Growth is all about thinking differently about things that were once difficult or confusing. It's like learning to ride a bike. The first time you are on the bike, you are terrified, but after you've fallen and skinned your knees and realized that it wasn't as painful as you thought, you resolve to figure out how to ride a bike or die trying. Then you learn to ride the bike, and voilà! Riding a bike has never been more fun! Now, imagine if you didn't ride the bike. Now, swap out the bike with something you've always wanted to do but are scared of starting. Every new skill or ability is learned, just like riding a bike. You can avoid the bike, and you'll never learn how to ride it. Or you can decide to enjoy the thrill of learning to ride and become proficient at riding. Choose to enjoy the process rather than get angry, frustrated, or worse yet, avoid trying new things that are valuable in terms of your success in life. Stop waiting. It always gets better.

CHAPTER 3: THE FALLACY OF PROFICIENCY

Your cleverness to adapt reflects on how you see challenges. If you continually do the same thing over and over again, which can cause boredom or frustration if you're failing, then it's on you to change something about the process to make it more enjoyable to you. The mentality of doing the same thing repeatedly and expecting a different result is the definition of insanity. But when you realize that your *initial* proficiency won't ultimately determine if you like something or not, it will cause you to get excited to start doing the things you "don't like." If the end result is valuable enough to you, then you will push through the initial failure required to develop proficiency in order to achieve the end result.

YOU CAN DO ANYTHING, BUT YOU CAN'T DO EVERYTHING

I am a believer that you can learn to be proficient at anything you *decide* to be proficient at, but you can't decide to be proficient at **everything**. You simply don't have enough time in your life to be excellent at everything you do. So, how do you know what skills you should spend your time developing proficiency? Here is the exact process you should go through to know where to spend your time. I use this same process with all of my consulting clients and it works wonders.

First, identify or remind yourself of your top ten life goals. There are some great tools to help you organize and think through your goals and thoughts in the free resources workbook that you can scan below to help you get started. I recommend using the BE/DO/HAVE list and the DREAM LIST to put your goals into focus. Keep in mind that figuring out your goals in life can be quite tricky, and it will take you longer than most exercises. But once you have them, they will help you direct your efforts for the rest of your life!

Once you have your goals clearly identified, ask yourself what steps you will have to take to accomplish them. Map out or reverse engineer, every step that you think you will have to take in order to reach your goals. And I use the word "think" here because, undoubtedly, you won't know every single step of the way at the time of creating these steps. There are almost always more steps than you first realize when doing this exercise.

Finally, identify your strengths and weaknesses. Why? While you can learn to enjoy challenging yourself to develop proficiency, you also have particular natural strengths and weaknesses to consider. An excellent book listed on the recommended resources page of the workbook called *StrengthsFinders 2.0®* from Gallup® and Tom Rath includes the CliftonStrengths Finders test within their book. I highly recommend buying and using this resource to identify your top five strengths and learn about your weaknesses. You will find in life that you can grow your top five strengths almost limitlessly while no matter how hard you try to grow your weaknesses, you will hit a limit to your capabilities.

CHAPTER 3: THE FALLACY OF PROFICIENCY

When you combine your personal goals for your life and the steps you need to take in order to reach those goals with your strengths in mind, you can start to identify the activities you need to start spending your time on and the activities that you don't. For example, if you have the strength of winning others over and you want to build a business, then you should spend your time winning others over. If you have a weakness of organization, you should build a team around you and surround yourself with people who have strengths in organization so your business can stay organized and grow. Don't fall into the trap that you have to *be good at everything*. In fact, because there is so little time and so many things, this is impossible to do. Instead, identify where you want to go, your goals, and the steps you need to take. Then, figure out which steps you will be best at taking and find others to help with the rest! Usually, these others will have the same goals as you do. When you meet them and begin working together, nothing will stop you from reaching those goals.

DEVELOPING PROFICIENCY

When you start learning something new to take steps towards your ultimate goals in life, you can't get any worse than you'll be on your first try. Therefore, the more time you put into the task, the more your confidence will grow as you become more *proficient*. Your mind will develop habits around that task and you'll probably enjoy things more as they become easier to do. After this process, you will enjoy what you are doing! How funny is that?

THE PROBLEM WITH POTENTIAL

What I've found in my unique experience of over 7,000 hours of door-to-door sales—and recruiting forty-three people to do the same thing—is that the number one reason people procrastinate doing what's important and valuable to them is because they don't like to do those things. They don't feel proficient *yet*. How many times have you heard someone decide not to do something because they "don't like it?" How many people avoid asking for what they want because they don't like rejection? But how does one ever get what they want if they never ask? How many people don't try something new because they think they will fail?

This avoidance mentality is often socialized into commonality. I can remember many moments in high school, college, and at my previous jobs when people would gather around the break room or study room and would spend time talking about all the things they didn't like about what they were currently doing. By talking about it, they bounced their ideas off a soundboard of agreement as the group nodded to each other about how unmotivated they were to accomplish the seemingly meaningless work in front of them. As they procrastinated doing the work they didn't like, the work started to pile up. Then, near the final deadline, the group would pull together and finish the work just in time with a lot more stress than was needed. In fact, they were so angry that they would often sink into victimhood! "Why do I have to do all the work?"

CHAPTER 3: THE FALLACY OF PROFICIENCY

The human mind is wired to avoid pain and frustration. New tasks require effort, focus, and conscious thoughts to develop new mental patterns. This takes energy, and there is always an uphill battle on the learning curve to become proficient. The quicker you get started, the faster you will develop competency. This mental pattern is what I call *the fallacy of proficiency*: the erroneous belief that we must already be good at a task to work on it, enjoy it, or be excited about it before we *start*. The *fallacy of proficiency* is the leading cause of procrastination because your potential for extraordinary achievement requires you to *start* to learn things that you don't know how to do. That is why it is called potential, after all. It's not yet achieved. But it will be if you take the necessary steps. If you want to be the best version of yourself and achieve great things, you must confront this fallacy and work against it.

THE STORY OF VIKTOR FRANKL

In the book *Man's Search for Meaning*, the author, Viktor Frankl, is a Jew imprisoned in the death camps in Nazi Germany, just as he was in real life. He had the worst situation in all of human history. There is nothing more atrocious than what was being done in the death camps. According to holocaust.com, of the nearly 10-million Jews in Europe at the beginning of World War II, 5.7-million died in the Holocaust. Nearly 60% of all Jews were murdered at the hands of the Nazis. Viktor was one of the few survivors.[9]

---

[9] *The Nazi Genocide Against the Jewish People*. (2018, October 17). TheHolocaust.com. https://holocaust.com.au/

THE PROBLEM WITH POTENTIAL

Before the war Viktor was a neurologist and psychologist. After he was freed, he wrote about his experiences and observances. For his book, he studied the human mind and observed the most brutal punishment the mind could ever suffer through and survive. He was malnourished. He was beaten. He no longer had a name but was called by a prisoner number. He witnessed countless deaths of his fellow Jews as the Nazis attempted to murder an entire people.

He described his observations of how long people would survive or struggle in the camps. He witnessed people who quite literally shouldn't have medically survived, based on starvation and malnutrition, push through these conditions because they *needed* to survive to see their loved ones on the outside. He also witnessed many prisoners who had no reason to live, and they quickly withered away. Viktor is a man to be remembered, as are all of those fateful souls who were murdered in World War II. His purpose at the time was to survive the ordeal to share with the world what had happened in remembrance of the atrocities in those camps. He had a purpose to survive and has changed the world because of it. He concluded that your mindset was everything, and the mind needed a purpose to survive.

Purpose dictates how you live and your enthusiasm for living. If you see a purpose for what you are doing, you will be more motivated to do it even if it's difficult or painful. Think of all the stories of mothers lifting vehicles off the ground to save a

CHAPTER 3: THE FALLACY OF PROFICIENCY

baby. Frankl was never willing to give up because he needed to share what happened with the world. The world needed to know firsthand what evil had been conducted by the Nazis. He decided that no matter what came his way, he would survive. He would live. He decided to endure his circumstances, no matter how painful or difficult it was, because he needed to survive so this would never happen again.

If you can assign value to a task because it is worth it to you, then why wouldn't you decide to like it? Go one step further; why wouldn't you pick things that are good for you instead of relegating yourself to never doing them from an internal decision to "not like" that thing? The average person decides not to like things that are good for them because they unintentionally believe in the fallacy of proficiency.

In this thought process, one might think they must have natural talent to enjoy a task. By definition, the fallacy of proficiency places value only on the short-term pleasure of a task or activity instead of the long-term gain of the task. This short-term pain causes many to avoid specific tasks based on their natural talent to be "good" rather than what will result.

Your natural excitement about something is directly related to how good you are at that particular task because you feel confident doing it, especially compared to those around you. This confidence and developed proficiency are directly related to the time and effort you've spent focusing on becoming good at the task. This means what you enjoy about the tasks you are good at is that you have already gone through the difficult learning curve to turn that task into a habit where you don't have to think about the task consciously. So, in truth, whether you like something or not, you are led to believe some things aren't for you simply because you have not put in enough time or effort to become proficient at that thing—which often leads to limiting beliefs, low confidence, and limited achievements. On the other hand, for those who are naturally gifted and talented in many areas, the lack of effort to become successful at whatever talent one can develops limits of complacency. This is where talent becomes a curse. When you rely on talent, you often don't build the proper mental toughness to find excitement in overcoming new learning curves. When you are talented and learning is easy, there are very few setbacks, which develops a mindset that learning new things is easy until they aren't. If you rely on talent, then when you want to learn to do something that you aren't talented at, there is a strong chance that you will fall into the fallacy of proficiency and avoid the new task.

THE READING EXAMPLE

The fallacy of proficiency develops at startlingly young ages, and once habitual in our thinking, it is difficult to overcome. Let's look at many Americans' shared dislike as an example. According to WordsRated in 2022, 51.57% of Americans hadn't read a book in over a year. I am also assuming these

CHAPTER 3: THE FALLACY OF PROFICIENCY

statistics include audiobooks. If this is true, that would mean that 51.57% of people *dislike* reading—or find reading tedious, or difficult to start, or, at the very least, don't prioritize reading. For the sake of this example, since I cannot perceive the countless reasons why 51.57% of people don't read, let's just use this one possible reason that reading isn't *fun*.

Now, the benefits of reading are countless. Studies show that reading can reduce stress by 68%. **Ten** Studies also show that reading at least six minutes daily can improve your sleep quality and sharpen your mental acuity. Not to mention that you also learn how to solve life's many problems, learn about cultures, and enjoy the creativity of another human being's mind. So, reading has many benefits, like many other habits we choose to avoid.[10]

Imagine you are a six-year-old learning to read; let's say that you've spent less time practicing reading with your parents, for whatever reason. With less practice, you may struggle with sounding out words or reading comprehension of what is on the page. You are then placed in a classroom and see that others are already good at reading when compared with your own skills. You begin to compare yourself to your peers. Seeing that you are not as skilled, you become embarrassed and frustrated, asking yourself, "Is something wrong with me?" There is a negative emotional response to this situation

---

10 Rizzo, N. *Over 50% of Americans Haven't Read a Book in the Past Year*. (2023, May 26). WordsRated. https://wordsrated.com/american-reading-habits-study/

of embarrassment. After that, every time reading is brought up, you don't want to read because reading not only is challenging, but it also brings up the negative emotional response you felt in the classroom when you compared yourself to fellow classmates.

This is a template for developing low confidence and dislikes that cause you to avoid challenging yourself. A comparison like this makes you judge yourself in ways you don't even realize, leaving you with specific emotional memories that flare up when you need to perform in front of others. And if you allow those emotions to flare up when you are trying to succeed and fail because of distracting negative memories, you might fail in the moment. Each failure can snowball into believing you will fail in the future, which could cause you to avoid trying again. If you don't try again to counteract that experience, you will interpret each failure as something wrong with you, leading to an even more negative image of yourself. The only answer to growing past this comparison is to deal with this problem head-on.

Overcoming this natural thought process of needing to be good at something to enjoy it—or start learning to improve your proficiency—is integral to reaching your potential. When you start understanding that you can train your mind to assign value to otherwise monotonous tasks based on your purpose and goals, you will realize that you can develop proficiency at almost anything! Isn't that an incredibly freeing feeling? Once you've truly accepted this fact, you can stop overthinking and start taking action toward reaching your true potential in life.

THE COMPARISON OF PROFICIENCY

Apply this template to any other skill you've ever heard of. You can see that the mind develops limits on itself through *comparison of proficiency*. Because of this, the *fallacy of proficiency* is born in your mind, and you start to believe that you only like or find value in things that you are good at or have come most easily to you. As you grow past the fallacy, you will start to look at complex tasks as fun challenges to be overcome because you can learn them and because they help you reach your goals, meaning they are valuable. You want to train your mind to enjoy the process of learning to be good at things rather than enjoying the results of being good at things because of talent. As you might expect, continuing this old mental habit from childhood will hinder your personal growth. You must face this problem and come to terms with the fallacy of comparison and proficiency. The good news is that you are in charge of your mind and life, and you can decide what matters to you. Be proud of your accomplishments and progress; and do your best to stop comparing yourself to others in pursuing your goals in life.

The above is a beautiful theory, accurate, and it works, but growth isn't what you understand. It's about what you apply. Overcoming the fallacy of proficiency is a slow process at first. Because when you start, you get a lot of negative feedback. Unfortunately, others may not know about the fallacy of proficiency; therefore, they still believe in the old mindset of comparing their skills to others to feel confident. This means that many people will judge you if you struggle when you are learning something new. This cycle of external feedback that can influence you into believing what others think about you is called the Pygmalion effect. The Pygmalion effect is the idea that your actions are influenced by what you *believe* and that what you *believe* about yourself is influenced by those around you. This is played out when someone makes fun of you for not being good at something and will be covered much more thoroughly in Chapter 5.

When you are made fun of, it's easy to avoid focusing on developing the habit or skill you are working on because of the negative emotions from feeling inferior. But this is part of life! If you want to grow, you will experience growing pains. At some point, you have to decide that it is worth more to you to step out from the norms of what is acceptable to become proficient at any task or skill that is important to you, **regardless of what others think.**

THE STORY OF DAVID GOGGINS

In 1994 a man named David Goggins started his career with

CHAPTER 3: THE FALLACY OF PROFICIENCY

the US Air Force. As he was going through training, he quit pararescue school. Goggins wasn't proficient in the water. He said he hated being in the water! Then, the military doctors told him he had a blood disease and wouldn't have to continue these intense missions if he didn't want to due to the illness. At the time, Goggins didn't want to continue, so he was transferred to become a tactical air controller for the rest of his contract. Goggins said, "It gave me a way out. I didn't want to go back in the water, so I pretty much just quit."

Goggins said the fact that he dropped out of pararescue school depressed him, and due to this, he began to let himself go and gain weight until he exited active-duty service. His next job was pest control where he sprayed cockroaches. Unfortunately, he continued to gain weight and lose confidence and motivation. At one point he weighed 297 pounds.

While working pest control, Goggins decided to watch a documentary on the Navy SEALs' Hell Week. As a result, he became inspired to do more. He believed that he could do something big, and he wanted to become a Navy SEAL. His current weight, lack of fitness, and lack of accolades didn't stop him. He knew he needed to change. He needed to do something with his life.

Goggins said the following in a podcast interview about that time: "I'm tired of feeling the way I feel every day… Tired of lying to myself, lying to people, and just being some piece of shit. And I always knew in the back of my mind, I could be something special, but I knew the work [that] it was going to take would kill me. I was afraid of that. I was afraid of that brutality in the suffering [that] I was going to have to endure, but I knew, I knew I could do something..."[11]

When Goggins aspired to join the Navy SEALs, he was far from the weight standards, and he was older than most Navy SEALs. Goggins called a lot of recruiters. Most of them hung up on him after hearing how much he weighed. Finally, one recruiter gave him a chance, and if he could lose 106 pounds in three months, he would allow him to attempt the BUD/s training that all Navy SEALs must pass to become a SEAL. BUD/s was intense training. These Navy SEAL hopefuls would have to run countless miles and endure sleepless nights where instructors tried to make them quit. Goggins would go through the most challenging training in the American armed forces and do whatever it took, even when so many others failed. In fact, during the hardest week of training, aptly named Hell Week, he broke his kneecap and still finished the training so he wouldn't be disqualified. That is mental toughness.

Unfortunately, he couldn't keep up with his class, so after two weeks, he was sent back to restart once his knee was healed. Passing BUD/s took him three attempts which means he failed twice. He wasn't the best on his first try. He didn't succeed at first, but he developed a mindset to succeed. If you follow Goggins past his military career, he has now

---

[11] Mylett, E. (Host). (2019, July 30) *Victory in Suffering—with David Goggins*. (Ep. 7 The Ed Mylett Show. https://www.edmylett.com/podcast/david-goggins-victory-in-suffering

CHAPTER 3: THE FALLACY OF PROFICIENCY

completed over sixty ultramarathons, many of which were over 100-mile races, and he holds the Guinness world record for pull-ups at 4,030 pull-ups in seventeen hours.

Goggins started at 297 pounds, depressed, and feeling like a failure, but he wanted to be more. He worked to achieve incredible things and reach his potential. He wasn't the best athlete or the toughest mentally when he started, but he set a goal and did whatever it took to achieve it. Regardless of where you start or what mistakes you have made, what you want to do is possible; it may just appear impossible. You don't have to be great to start. You just have to be willing to learn and do whatever it takes to succeed, including pushing through pain.[12]

I remember when I was thirteen years old. I wanted to learn how to play the guitar to impress the ladies. I just knew that girls would flock to me in high school if I could learn the guitar! So, I resolved to learn this new skill. My mom had played and was a good singer, so naturally, I figured I could learn to do the same. I started playing, and I suddenly realized that pushing down guitar strings hurt like crazy, and the strings made your fingertips feel like they were bleeding and on fire simultaneously! It wasn't fun, and then I realized how uncoordinated I was! I couldn't strum with my right hand, let alone find the places for my fingers to go with my

---

12 Rooney, A. (*The Toughest Man Alive*. 2018, November 27). U.S. Navy - All Hands. https://allhands.navy.mil/Stories/Display-Story/Article/1840612/the-toughest-man-alive/

THE PROBLEM WITH POTENTIAL

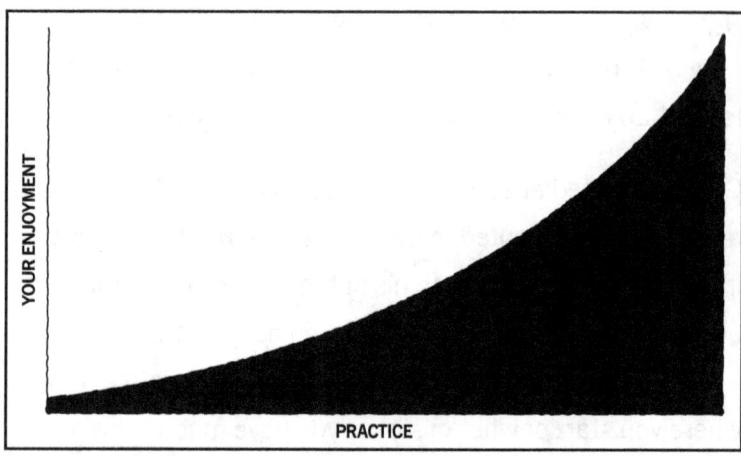

Figure 3.1: As you practice something, you become more proficient. The more proficient you are, the more you enjoy that activity.

left hand when I wasn't strumming. I was a total mess. After a couple of weeks, I gave up. I felt so embarrassed because I just felt like I sounded terrible. I only played in my room because I feared people hearing my lousy playing. I had it all in my head that my brothers were making fun of me, and I made myself extremely sensitive to even good-hearted questions about how it was coming along. I made up a story in my head that they were judging me even when they were just asking me a question.

About a year later, I resolved to play again after a church conference I went to. I wanted to learn how to play to play Christian songs and worship alone in my room. My fire to learn had been ignited, and I started playing daily, watching YouTube video lessons to learn songs and techniques faster. I

CHAPTER 3: THE FALLACY OF PROFICIENCY

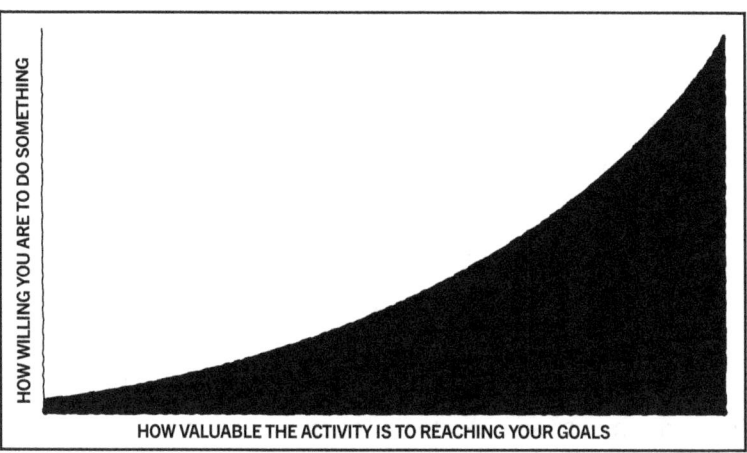

Figure 3.2: How willing or excited you are to do an activity is a direct correlation with how valuable the activity is to reaching your goals. It has little to do with what you like or dislike.

mastered a few songs and have been playing ever since!

You see, the first time I tried playing guitar, I focused on trying to sound good to be attractive to girls, while the second time around, I only focused on developing a skill that meant more to me than external stimulus. I was learning because I genuinely enjoyed the *process* of getting better and the sweet sound of music! The second time around, I overcame my fears of being overheard and even played in the living room while others went about their activities. I learned to not care, and I realized that they barely even noticed me anyway. As it turns out, you think more about yourself than anyone around you.

The reason I was learning the guitar was so strong that nothing and no one could stop me from figuring it out, and I promise that when I started playing again, I was no better than when I had stopped. The only thing that changed was my mindset. I *decided* that being good wasn't the point. The point was to learn how to do something because I *enjoyed* it. I mean, playing music is incredible! At some point in my learning to play, I chose to enjoy the guitar. I changed my outlook on the people around me and disarmed them with their unintentionally hurtful words.

You must push through the fear of rejection and not care if you are bad at something to become good at it. Unless you are a prodigy, be encouraged by the fact that you and everyone else are comparatively bad at everything you try for the first time. So, if you think about it, anyone making fun of you used to be bad at the same things you struggle with. They've just forgotten that they started poorly because human beings like to forget moments of failure whenever possible. Honestly, who "wants" to remember when you sucked at something? You can be encouraged by the fact that the people who make fun of others aren't trying to hurt people. They may not yet have enough self-awareness to realize why they are doing because very few people intentionally reflect on their identity and actions. Therefore, they make emotionally driven and impulsive decisions to make fun of people. It's all a cycle fueled by emotionally driven and impulsive decision-making. If there is anything you should focus on when learning a new skill, it is this: your success in any endeavor isn't whether you start off being good or bad; your willingness to control your emotions, see the bigger

CHAPTER 3: THE FALLACY OF PROFICIENCY

picture, and never give up—no matter how hard it gets—determines your success in any endeavor.

Now, imagine if every time you tried to take a step towards reaching your goals, something difficult came up. Instead of pushing through, you give up when the going gets tough. When you give up, your dreams don't change. Your desires don't change. You change. You develop a habit of quitting when things are difficult. This causes procrastination. The longer you procrastinate, the less likely you will ever take a step towards achieving your goals and potential. And if you never start, you will never reach your true potential.

Everyone gets stuck in their head. We all have fears and insecurities that bounce around our minds like an endless game of tennis. We often don't even remember why they exist in our brains or when they started! But at some point, when you were just minding your own business, something created a block in your mind, originating from a memory of failure or pain that sticks with you. This moment can develop a personal belief about yourself that can start the trend of giving up on trying new things because you've convinced yourself that they are either too difficult to complete or you are not good enough to learn them. But it doesn't have to be this way. Action cures fear. Action conquers these negative thoughts because through actions, repetition, and eventually success, you prove that your past thoughts about yourself are incorrect.

Now, ask yourself this: how many things are you avoiding

THE PROBLEM WITH POTENTIAL

because they are difficult or uncomfortable? That thought can be overwhelming. What do you LOVE doing that you avoid because you think you aren't good enough at it? If you love it, don't fall for the fallacy of proficiency, where you think you have to be good at it to like it. Remember that everyone is not proficient when they start. In fact, they aren't very good at all. Suppose you incorporate the mentality that you decide what you like and you stop caring what others think. In that case, you will start seeing new challenges as a necessary and exciting process you must go through to grow. The exact method for growth in one area is the same for growth in every aspect of life. The difference is the unique information or actions for each particular skill or result. Deciding to enjoy short-term challenges will inspire you to take actionable steps toward reaching your goals and doing what you love. All you have to do is get started.

CHAPTER 4
THE LAW OF DIMINISHING POTENTIAL

A winner is a dreamer who never gives up.

—Nelson Mandela

Nelson Mandela was born in the small village of Mvezo on July 18, 1918. In 1942, he began entering the world of politics in South Africa. He graduated college at the University of South Africa in 1943 and soon after achieved a two-year diploma to practice law. During the next twenty or so years, Mandela tried to help with the movement to create equality in his country by abolishing racist laws, known as apartheid, so that everyone could live in harmony in South Africa. In 1964, Mandela was on trial because he was protesting the Apartheid regime, and he was sentenced to life in prison because of this political stance and accused of alleged incitement and sabotage. At the trial, Mandela famously said, "I have fought against white domination, and I have fought against black domination. I have cherished the ideal of a democratic and free society in which all people live together in harmony and with equal opportunities. It is an ideal that I hope to live for and to achieve. But if needs be, it is an ideal for which I am prepared to die."

Nelson Mandela was sentenced to five years in prison in 1962. In 1964, Mandela was given a life sentence and stayed in prison until 1990. That's twenty-six years imprisoned in a tiny cell, often with no plumbing or bed. They offered to release him early on three separate occasions, but he would not leave until every last person who was wrongfully thrown in jail for political beliefs was set free. Soon after, Mandela ran for president, and on May 10, 1994, he became the first democratically elected president in South African history. Mandela turned eighty in 1998. He was one of the oldest presidents to have ever served in government. In 2013, he died at the age of ninety-five, still working towards making South Africa a better place.[13]

A WINNER IS A DREAMER WHO NEVER GIVES UP

A winner is a dreamer who never gives up. Nelson Mandela lived this out his entire life by working hard towards making

---

[13] *Biography of Nelson Mandela*. (n.d.). Nelson Mandela Foundation. https://www.nelsonmandela.org/content/page/biography

CHAPTER 4: THE LAW OF DIMINISHING POTENTIAL

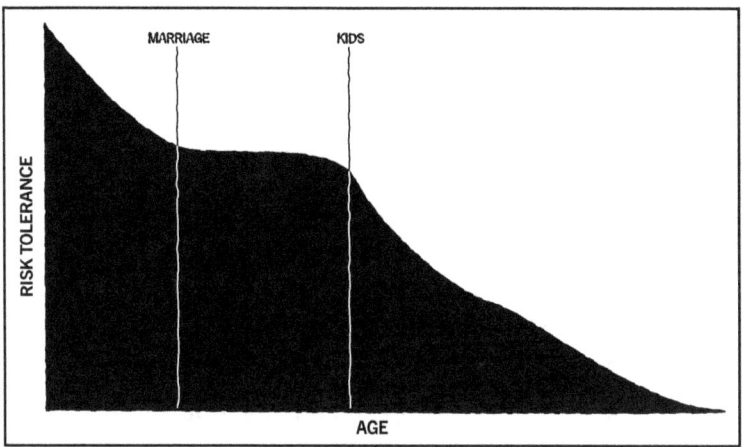

Figure 4.1: As you age, you take on more responsibilty which lowers your risk tolerance, not your ability to do big things or make an impact.

the world a better place. In 1993, he even won the Nobel Peace Prize in his seventies. His age did not define his ability nor limit his ability to effect change in the world. He didn't allow himself to be limited by the law of diminishing potential; in fact, he is the exception to the rule everyone should strive to be, as age doesn't limit your potential impact on others and the world.

The law of diminishing potential represents the expected change in risk tolerance as your age increases: your willingness to take risks decreases, and therefore, your potential diminishes. Your potential doesn't diminish because you have less time; as you grow, you will develop a higher skill level, broader connections, and status in the world that help you make things happen at a much higher rate than a young person who is just starting in life. Your potential diminishes as

THE PROBLEM WITH POTENTIAL

you age because you become *less likely* to take risks. As you age, your willingness to take risks decreases because of the increase in your fear of failure. This mentality is quite natural when you think about it and is not objectively wrong. Still, it is essential to understand why you might be holding yourself back from extraordinary results and impacting more people.

When you are young, you have no one to take care of except yourself (most of the time). This means you can go and fail at something and get back up and try again with little to no consequences. You naturally have more energy when you are young, and you have more freedom to make new commitments, as you don't have as many previous responsibilities to attend to and, often, you aren't married with children, *yet*. As you age, you become comfortable in your life and what you have built, so you avoid "messing that up." Essentially, you can often settle for "second best" by saying no to the one thing you wish you were doing.

According to a poll conducted by Gallup in 2019, only 15% of employees are engaged at work, meaning 85% don't like their jobs. Why on earth would anyone submit to hating their job if there were steps they could take to change what they were doing? After all, you spend about 33% of your life working, so why not do something you love?[14]

---

[14] Clarisse. *Why 85% of People Hate Their Jobs*. (2019, December 21). Staff Squared. https://staffsquared.com/blog/why-85-of-people-hate-their-jobs/

CHAPTER 4: THE LAW OF DIMINISHING POTENTIAL

Once you are stuck in a job you don't like but it "pays the bills," it is quite hard to change. I believe that every one of us has a deep desire to do the best we can in life. Most don't want to reflect on our lives and say, "It could have been me." No one wants to look back on their life with regrets, but so many people do this very thing.

If you commit to and go after your dreams no matter what it takes, naturally, over time, you will develop more skills, connections, and abilities. Your dream, over time, will become a reality. How much time it will take depends on your skills, abilities, and the hours you put in. Age doesn't matter.

There were two lumberjacks chopping wood in the forest. The first lumberjack was young and inexperienced but very motivated, and he started chopping wood at 7:00 a.m. and chopped straight through until 7:00 p.m. The second lumberjack was older but more experienced. He started at 7:00 a.m., chopped wood until noon, and returned at 2:00 p.m. He then chopped wood until 6:00 p.m. and went home. Both lumberjacks chopped the same amount of wood every single day. After a few weeks of this, the first lumberjack was exhausted and angry. He was furious at the other lumberjack because he was working less AND coming up with the same result as he was. How could this be? What was he doing wrong? So, the lumberjack swallowed his pride, and his curiosity overwhelmed him. He finally asked the second lumberjack, "How do you cut as much wood as I do, but you don't even work as hard as me?" The second lumberjack smiled humbly and replied, "When I take a break, I go home, refuel, and sharpen my axe."

This is a parable I use with all of my consulting clients to help them understand that work ethic isn't the only input to a successful business or a successful life. Sharpening your axe is just as crucial as an unshakable work ethic. Sharpening your axe means improving your effectiveness to perform better with every swing.

In addition to this idea, you can see that the young lumberjack has lots of energy but less experience and relies on work ethic. In contrast, the older lumberjack relies on experience and technique. Both can accomplish similarly big things, but only if they consistently put in effort. That is why wherever you are, you should start taking actionable steps towards your goals and dreams as soon as possible.

BE INTENTIONAL

The law of diminishing potential is similar to the 10,000-hour rule. The 10,000-hour rule is the idea that it takes 10,000 hours to become a master at anything. Supposing this is true, as you age, you have more responsibility with your current job, spouse, kids, etc. Spending hours developing the skill you care about becomes more complex, so starting now is almost always the best choice. If becoming a master is a simple math problem of inputting enough time, then all you need to do is start consis-

CHAPTER 4: THE LAW OF DIMINISHING POTENTIAL

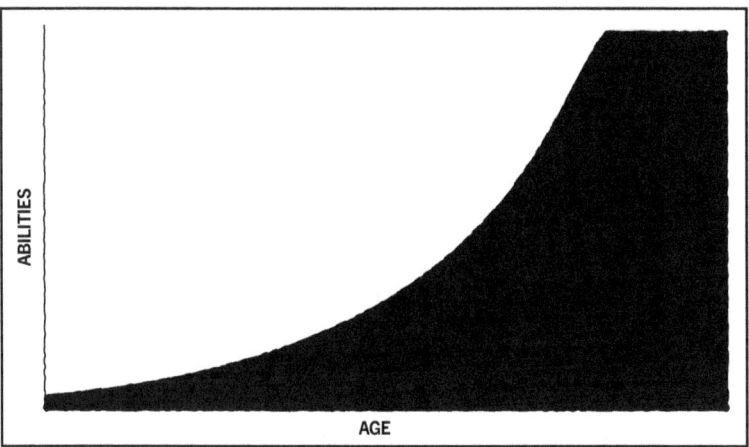

Figure 4.2: As you age, your abilities grow exponentially due to your life experience.

tently putting in time to become more experienced. As you grow, your time investment will change from the first lumberjack to the second as you learn ways to improve. The only caveat is that you will have less time to work on the most important tasks as you often have more commitments, which diminishes your potential **if and only if <u>you aren't intentional with your time.</u>**

Being intentional with your time is simple but not easy. There will be a million "fires" to put out daily at work, with your family, or with your obligations. Regardless of these urgent and important duties, you must find a way to prioritize what is important to you rather than saying yes to every opportunity that comes up. In the lumberjack example, the lumberjack sharpened his axe and continued to chop wood. He was more efficient with his time, allowing him to rest more or do other valuable activities. He created time freedom from his job by being more thoughtful about approaching the job. Because he was intentional with his education, he could open more possibilities to do whatever he felt called to do.

For example, I think our society puts too much emphasis on "kids being a distraction" from reaching your potential in life. And I just disagree. When you are raising children, you are leaving a legacy. In the example of the lumberjack, he was successful at what he did at work, but he also had more time to go home. I like to imagine that he probably had a family with kids.

You don't have to be the topmost professionally or financially successful person to be happy or reach your potential. Your goal might be that you want to have an incredible family. And leading and building an incredibly happy family would be fulfilling your potential! I would also venture to say that you can have a great family and still help many people outside of the home and that you ought to pursue helping those people! So don't get distracted by external societal pressures and forget about what really matters. When I'm talking about being intentional with your time, I'm talking about figuring out ways to make consistent progress towards whatever goals and priorities you have so you can impact more people.

Whatever your situation, you can make time to take actual steps toward reaching your potential. The mistake is that people often become too intense. They do a great job by taking steps toward goals, but they only work in sporadic large chunks rather than consistent small ones. In fact, realize that you can't force growth to happen faster than your habits and mind can keep up with, so slow down and just keep taking steps.

Studies show that intense studying, or cramming, does not lead to long-term memory storage. This means cramming's only result is short-term memory for a moment, not a lifetime. The information learned will dissipate rapidly and become unusable. What's better is dedicating just an hour a day towards learning or working towards your goals. Whether it's to be more impactful at work or leave a better legacy at home, everyone has an hour to focus, no matter your situation. Remember, consistency is more valuable than intensity, and proper growth comes over a much more extended period than we expect.

BE SOLUTION-FOCUSED

When distractions or problems arise, focus on solutions and avoid the lure of "acceptable" excuses. If you allow something to get in your way, it will be in your way. Instead, be solutions-focused. This means that when a problem presents itself, you don't linger on it or complain that it exists, but rather, you see the problem and ask, "How can this be solved?" You don't pout. You don't get angry. You accept the situation for what it is, and you solve it. Therefore, no matter your roadblocks, there is a solution; all you have to do is find it. Everyone has wasted time when they aren't doing something important. Only a few people could even claim they are too busy to achieve their dreams. In reality, if you think you are too busy to reach your potential, it's because you are likely prioritizing things that don't matter to you over things that do matter to you. Bob Goff, one of my favorite authors of all time, said in his book *Love Does*, "I used to be afraid of failing at things that matter. Now I'm afraid to succeed at things that don't matter."

Anyone can make the excuse of time, but few reflect and realize that those who make this excuse are just *unorganized* with their time. Regardless of what you've been doing, you need to start now.

When you are taking the first steps to start, you may be tempted to fall into the comparison trap and start looking around at other already successful people in the area you want to succeed. This is normal, and this problem must be met head-on. The Singer Example shows how it will feel, so you can realize it is normal. You will be less discouraged when you have proper expectations of what will happen.

THE SINGER EXAMPLE

Imagine you want to be a singer when you are ten, BUT you put it off until you're eleven. You then sing with all the kids that are eleven, and you are the worst because you've practiced for one year less. It is not because you are untalented, but rather unpracticed. The other singers have a year of more experience than you. You compare yourself to

CHAPTER 4: THE LAW OF DIMINISHING POTENTIAL

where their singing abilities and then conclude, "I'm not good enough." Even though singing is something you desperately want to do, you might put off this endeavor to avoid the pain of embarrassment. Then you try again at sixteen, and all the other hopeful singers have been singing for six years and you've been too scared to try. Then guess what? You compare yourself to six years of experience with the people around you, and you naturally begin to feel inferior to them. Comparatively, at this moment, you likely aren't as good as they are (unless you are a prodigy). The main reason they are better at this point is that they have simply put in more time. If you want to be a good singer, the answer is always to start now! You will always be uncomfortable and feel inadequate when you start something. And you will always grow past that feeling with enough practice. With more practice, your confidence increases. As your confidence increases, the comparison trap diminishes, and you start seeing better singing results and enjoy the activity more and more.

You push past these comparisons because you aren't pursuing singing, in this case, for the other people around you. You are doing it because you've always wanted to do it. You are doing it because it's a goal or dream that brings you joy, and you're tired of watching everyone else do what you know you're capable of. You don't always need to be the best! Of course, with enough practice, there's also nothing stopping you.

Regardless of this logic, you might find yourself stuck focusing on the short-term feelings of inadequacy. Therefore, you rationalize yet another excuse not to start singing because you don't think you're good enough. The goal isn't always to be the best; the goal is to become the best version of yourself. That means competing with yourself. If you aren't trying your best to reach your greatest potential in life, that's on you. No one else can stop you but yourself. What others do in life has very little to do with you, and comparing yourself almost always does one of the following unhealthy things to your mind. You either think you're better than everyone else, resulting in pride, and become egotistical. Or you see yourself as less compared to others, resulting in lower confidence and irrational, limiting beliefs. Comparison to others' proficiencies is nearly worthless in the pursuit of reaching your potential. This doesn't mean you don't look for worthy role models to strive for; in fact, you want to sing or do anything because you were inspired by someone else. I am saying that comparing your results to anyone else as you are trying to get started and actively pursuing them will keep you from reaching your potential.

So, just because you aren't good at something yet doesn't mean you can't be great. You might feel discouraged and rejected if you failed at anything in grade school, such as reading, math, science, or social encounters. Putting yourself out there is meant to make you feel this way, but you might have experienced these emotions in school, no matter the grade, because you wanted to fit in like everyone else. Other kids may have laughed at you if you didn't pronounce a word

CHAPTER 4: THE LAW OF DIMINISHING POTENTIAL

right when you read aloud because they were glad it was happening to you, and not them. Until now, you might not have looked at the big picture behind why they laughed at you at that point in life. All you perceived was that something negative like this happened to you; therefore, all you felt was rejection and humiliation due to your lack of proficiency.

DON'T LET EMBARRASSMENT HOLD YOU BACK

There are so many times in life where this similar pattern of embarrassment can occur, and often, you are left with negative emotions around certain activities involving your proficiency. If left unchecked, these moments can run together in your mind to create an identity surrounding failure and embarrassment. Your brain may start to believe that you can't do anything right, so why would you even try? From this point, your motivation to grow and leave your comfort zone can hit an all-time low. If you've felt this, you aren't alone. I would venture to say that this is a natural part of the human condition that nearly everyone experiences as they develop their identity. Avoid letting your identity crumble from these moments of failure and negative emotion by realizing that they are part of life and don't reflect your potential to be great. The first step in understanding this is looking at the bigger picture of why people make fun of others in the first place, and what leads to these moments happening. Once

THE PROBLEM WITH POTENTIAL

you know this, you will realize that when these things happen, people are unaware of their impact on others and aren't doing this for any reason other than conflict within themselves. If you were replaced with someone else, they would still do the same things to that person. It's never about you.

So, why do people make fun of others or ridicule others? This behavior starts with the culture's insistent indoctrination of the fear of failure. Social media and outward facades perpetuate the idea that every person imitates to look like they have their life all together. The truth is that no one is perfect. Everyone makes mistakes, and everyone needs help from time to time. Everyone has good and evil thoughts. Everyone is trying to grow. But, because everyone is trying to make you think that they have it all together, there is an intense fear of failure in front of others that leads to procrastination because there is a culturally normalized mentality of, "Why even try if you will probably fail?" Unfortunately, this is what leads to actual failure. Actual failure is giving up on something worth doing. It doesn't mean that you should never "quit" something. There is an excellent argument for quitting certain self-destructive habits and toxic relationships. Still, you ought not to give up on your dreams because it is difficult, and you might fail before becoming successful. This happens because many well-intentioned people with incredible potential misunderstand the difference between actual failure and "learning failure."

CHAPTER 4: THE LAW OF DIMINISHING POTENTIAL

LEARNING FAILURE

"Learning failure" is the failure every human *must* go through to learn something new. In learning failure, you learn by making mistakes, and then you perform better on the next try because you know what not to do. Because you know what not to do, you know how to improve upon what you are doing. You are learning through failure to become better. This makes such logical sense but, like many things, it is easier said than done. There is still social pressure to be perfect and people who will ridicule you when you fail. For some reason, people build up this mentality that we are *supposed* to be good at nearly everything on our first try. Unfortunately, it's nearly impossible to be good at everything. There just isn't enough time in the day to do everything.

You might be athletic due to years of sports, so picking up another sport may be easier due to your involvement in past athletic activities. However, picking up a new sport would be difficult if you have never competed. Your lack of experience would require climbing a much steeper learning curve. You must push through this natural part of life to unlock your potential. And it's true for nearly every occasion you learn something new. Action is the solution. Act, and you will improve. But how do you stop holding yourself back if you struggle to act?

THE PROBLEM WITH POTENTIAL

To get over this, you can reflect upon your perspective, and your mindset will reveal within you why you or others ridicule people when they fail.

For example, think about that last time you "made fun" of someone like the previous school examples. Did that add any value to their life? Well, why did you do it then?

When I did this growing up, I frequently wanted to make myself feel good, even if it came at the other person's expense. I didn't like the other person to be better than me at whatever they were doing. I wanted to be the best among my peers. I wanted to be confident that I was the best. At that time, I wasn't striving to be the best version of myself; I was falling into the comparison trap. This is also called an inferiority complex, which is when people want to avoid feeling inferior at all costs. I was projecting the fear of "learning failure" on the person I was making fun of so that I would feel good about myself.

COMPETE WITH YOURSELF

We all fall into this learning curve as well. I failed there, but I learned from it and try my best to avoid doing this at all costs throughout my life. Instead, I focus on competing with myself. If you don't focus on competing with yourself and striving for your best, then if you do happen to become the "best" at something among your peers, you will just stop trying. Why

CHAPTER 4: THE LAW OF DIMINISHING POTENTIAL

try if you are already on top? The comparison trap not only feeds your ego or feelings of inadequacy, but also limits your potential to the potential of people in proximity.

The inferiority complex is summed up in the time-honored phrase of the cynical and over-analytical person saying confidently, "That would never work because it's never been done before. It's impossible." But if you were to accomplish something the cynic is afraid of, they would feel uncomfortable because you did what they thought was impossible. No one likes to admit that they struggle with this thought pattern. And why would they? It's painful to realize, but if you never learn this, you will continue to discourage others, and you will continue to believe that some things are impossible. The best thing that can happen to cynics is for them to be proven wrong. Once they see that something is possible, he or she often accomplishes the same thing that they used to think was impossible. This is why you should never feel bad about doing well and going against the grain in these situations. Don't relegate yourself to mediocrity for fear of people with inferiority complexes making fun of you or feeling bad about themselves. After all, your success should inspire the success of others.

DON'T TRY TO FIT IN WITH EVERYONE

Everyone wants to feel important, and everyone wants to "fit in." It is human nature to desire approval and love. People are willing to do almost anything to get it! That's at the heart of the matter, but people get confused and hurt somewhere along the way, so they lash out because everyone else is doing the same thing. They become the product of their environment, allowing 10% of what happens to them to decide their thoughts instead of vice versa. Now that you know this, why doesn't everyone just jump on board with facing their failure? Because it's uncomfortable and it's risky.

People learn to stay "safe." The standard line of thought is often like this: "Don't dance because people will make fun of you. Don't sing because you can only sing if you sound good. Don't draw because it looks bad; others will make fun of you." These are *learned* fears. Remember when you were five? You were excellent at all these things. You could sing, dance, and draw; no matter the result, perfect or not, you were excited to try and show off your achievements. What would you do if you saw failure in the same light as a five-year-old?

Being successful is less about talent and more about action. It's not that you can't be good at whatever brings you joy. There's a point where you stop trying to be your best and reach your goals and dreams because you are **afraid to fail**. Your potential and success all come down to your mindset,

CHAPTER 4: THE LAW OF DIMINISHING POTENTIAL

which determines your actions. As the famous author Dale Carnegie once said, "Inaction breeds doubt and fear. Action breeds confidence and courage. If you want to conquer fear, do not sit at home and think about it. Go out and get busy."

You can unintentionally fix your mindset, causing you to believe that your actions are fixed. You have to be intentional with how you think so you can be intentional with your actions. If you want to change and unlock your potential, you must start getting your mind under control. Making it known is the best way to gain power over the unknown. By learning why your mind thinks the way it does and how it became that way, you can learn to control your mindset and change your actions to rewire your brain to overcome fear.

Unfortunately, this is an uphill battle because your brain is incredibly good at remembering particularly negative emotions. According to research done by Columbia University, "Humans often remember negative or traumatic experiences over positive ones."[15] Many scientists think this could be a survival defense mechanism built into our brains to help us avoid injury and painful circumstances. While great at helping us to remember to run from poisonous snakes or be wary when we are hiking a tall mountain, these natural processes can hold you back in the face of overcoming the very fear that hinders you from reaching your potential.

---

15 Harting, C. *How Can We Break the Cycle of Focusing on Negative Experiences?* (2022, March 9). Columbia News. https://tinyurl.com/breaknegativefocuscycle

THE PROBLEM WITH POTENTIAL

What's interesting about memories is that our mental bias, in nearly every case, shifts our past experiences to be more negative than they were.

Think about it; you can easily recall intense memories when you were ridiculed by others or moments of embarrassing failure. Imagine in high school that you took a weightlifting class and made an utter embarrassment of yourself lifting weights incorrectly. In an interview with the Washington Post, Dr. Laura Carstensen, a psychology professor at Stanford University, said, "Memories are fallible. Long-term memories are nearly always wrong."[16] Your memory becomes increasingly fuzzy as you age, but the emotions attached to the experience stay the same.

Without realizing it, you can often convince yourself that the situation was much worse than it was in reality. You can convince yourself that the experience was so horrible that your bias toward the negative emotion blows the whole memory out of proportion! Then, you have built up in your mind this worst-case scenario of something simple, such as what going to the gym for the first time would look like, causing you to feel anxious. The gym is just an example, but as human beings, we all do this with something, and often it holds us back from becoming the best version of ourselves. Living a life where every decision is based on fear isn't a way anyone wants to live.

---

16 Caren, A. *Why We Often Remember the Bad Better than the Good.* (2018, November 1). The Washington Post. https://www.washingtonpost.com/science/2018/11/01/why-we-often-remember-bad-better-than-good/

CHAPTER 4: THE LAW OF DIMINISHING POTENTIAL

YOU GROW THROUGH PAIN

Now imagine how hard it would be to go to a gym for the first time if you've never worked out before. You start looking around at all the other men or women, and then you discover very quickly that you don't look anywhere near as muscular or fit as them, and you have no idea where to start because you've never lifted before. You then have two options: leave this uncomfortable situation and cave to your emotions of comparison and embarrassment, OR get started working out. In moments like this, it is tempting to forget that the strongest person in the gym with huge muscles began just like you and EXPERIENCED the same thing. Isn't that a comforting thought? Insert any activity, skill, mindset, or result, and the process and choice to achieve success are the same.

So, just like how your muscles start small but grow from consistent, intentional, and focused effort from working out, your mind is a muscle and can grow or deteriorate similarly. What's important to realize is that whether you're five, fifteen, or fifty, it's never too late to start developing yourself to be the best version of yourself. If you're young, you may lack experience, but you have energy and a willingness to learn and improve yourself. If you are older, you have wisdom, experience, and even if you have a bit less energy, you are more effective from your experience. There is no excuse to not do your best with the time you have to achieve extraordinary results. When you give it your best, others will see, and maybe—just maybe—they will be inspired to do the same and you will begin a ripple effect of inspiration, growth, and helping others.

CHAPTER 5

IDENTITY INSPIRES ACTION

Be a person of relentless encouragement.
See others for who they can become, not for who they are.
And do the same for yourself.

Personal growth, unlocking your potential, and achieving extraordinary results have more to do with your mentality than natural-born talent or anything else. Understanding how your mentality has developed since childhood and throughout adulthood will help you learn to change and improve the negative habits in your life, and it will help you inspire action to build new and better habits to help you reach your potential. So, how do you know what your mentality is at the current moment? And how will you improve your mentality to a level that will help you unlock your potential? The two concepts are intertwined in everything that you do.

First, your mentality is determined by your identity, and your habits determine your identity. What slows people down from unlocking their potential and achieving extraordinary results is procrastination, which is a mental habit. Procrastination often occurs when there is a lack of clarity in your identity because your identity precedes your actions. Identity determines your actions because your identity determines your confidence, and your confidence determines how likely you are to do something. Your confidence, as mentioned in the previous chapter, is often based on what you have done in the past and how you've developed yourself in the competency of a specific task or skill. Of course, this leads to the fallacy of proficiency, causing procrastination. There is a psychological truth that you must understand to grow: If you believe you will be successful at something, you are more likely to put effort into trying that thing. In other words, to inspire action and overcome procrastination, you must adopt a growth mindset over a fixed mindset. You must start to believe in what is possible rather than what you've seen happen before.

CHAPTER 5: IDENTITY INSPIRES ACTION

THE RECORD NO ONE *THOUGHT* COULD BE BROKEN

Before 1954, no one ever thought running a mile in under four minutes was possible. Everyone believed that the four-minute-mile mark was the true limit of the human body's physical capability. Runners had been attempting to break a four-minute mile since 1886. Everyone was trying to do it, including the best coaches and athletes in the world. At the time, the experts believed that the only way to break the four-minute mile would be on a perfect day in perfect conditions: "A hard clay track, 68 degrees, with a boisterous crowd urging the runner on to his best-ever performance." Interestingly, on May 6, 1954, Roger Bannister broke the four-minute mile for the first time in recorded human history on a wet track in front of a tiny crowd in Oxford, England. After 68 years, someone finally broke the record. What followed was shocking. Just 46 days after the historic run, a runner from Australia, John Landy, broke the four-minute mark. Within a year, three other runners were under four minutes at the same exact race. The dominoes began to fall, and the four-minute mile became a thing of the past. Now, everyone was doing it. Bannister broke the belief barrier. Now, it was *expected* at the highest level to be running an under-four-minute mile.

During my first few years of door-to-door sales, I thought selling 10,000 units, or over $200,000 of educational books and apps, was impossible to do in twelve weeks. In the American division, no one had sold that much in years in a single summer selling season. On the other hand, the European division always had at least five to ten salespeople over 10,000 units. One year, they had a salesman sell 30,000 units, or around $600,000 in educational products, in a single season. It just seemed impossible. Then, one of the best salespeople finally sold 10,000 units. The next year, he did it again, alone. In the third year, I and a couple of others sold 10,000 units in the American division. He sold over 12,000 units, and I sold 11,869 units. Both of us were well over the 10,000-unit mark. The following year, over fifteen American salespeople, some under twenty-three years old, sold over 10,000 units. That year, I even did it in less overall selling time. An American even sold 15,000 units in the summer. It was now *expected* for the top salespeople to do the same each year.

Just like with running an under-four-minute mile, 10,000 units seemed impossible. But then, it was possible and repeatable. There were just different steps to take in training for a four-minute mile, just like there was a different process for selling 10,000 or even 30,000 units in the summer. There is always a way to accomplish your goals. All it takes is one person to pioneer a process. Then, you can replicate the results. You may be that one person, or you want to do something that has already been done that seems impossible to most. Regardless of your goals, breaking your personal belief barriers works the same in anything you do. You must

CHAPTER 5: IDENTITY INSPIRES ACTION

buy into the idea that everything you want to do is achievable. There isn't a limit that can't be broken; there are only limits you believe can't. If it has been done before, it can be done again. If it hasn't been done before, someone will be the first. Believing that you can achieve what you put your mind to is called having a growth mindset.

A growth mindset is the idea that you can grow past any challenge. Challenges are fun to attempt, as a challenge requires you to think differently and find new ways to tackle problems. By overcoming these challenges, you better understand yourself, the world, and your capabilities to succeed. A fixed mindset is the exact opposite. A fixed mindset is the idea that you are born the way you are and are only good at what you have been good at since birth. Therefore, there's no point in trying new things. There's no evidence to **believe** that you can become better; therefore, the mentality arises that other people are just more talented than you and that's the way it is. Your abilities and mentality are fixed.

Interestingly enough, a large percentage of people have convinced themselves that they are the way they are, and there isn't much they can do about it. They believe they are either naturally talented or weren't meant to be good at something. *Big Life Journal's* article about author Carol Dweck states, "As many as 40% of students have a fixed versus growth mindset."[17] These children often: give up quickly and

---

17 Louick, R. Growth Mindset vs. Fixed Mindset: Key Differences and How to Shift Your Child's Mindset. (2023, June 25). Big Life Journal. https://tinyurl.com/shiftyourchildsmindset

easily; dislike and resent the progress and growth of their classmates; and feel intense pressure to prove their worth over and over. In Dweck's book *Mindset: The New Psychology of Success*, she talks about how "looking" smart to the fixed mindset person is more important than actual learning. This mentality is in conflict with learning failure. You have to fail to learn. You have to get outside of the box. You have to break away from the false dichotomy that you are either "naturally talented" or you just "aren't good at some things." And as an adult, you've brought these same habits with you.

FALSE DICHOTOMIES

A dichotomy is two things that are in opposition. A false dichotomy is the idea that there are only two possible mutually exclusive outcomes, when in reality, you can get both, or there are more options, such as a third, fourth, or more that you didn't even think about. False dichotomies create fear, and they limit you to living in only one or two ways. In truth, there are often multiple and sometimes limitless options for how to tackle problems. False dichotomies are developed in your mind based on your knowledge gaps. False dichotomies are created from a lack of **belief** in what is possible because you don't know the extent of what is truly possible.

For example, imagine if you lived your entire life thinking that the only two options for work were either working at McDon-

CHAPTER 5: IDENTITY INSPIRES ACTION

ald's or working at Walmart. And imagine you were absolutely convinced that there was no other option than these two jobs. In fact, these were the best two opportunities on the planet. Logically, left with two options, you would do your best to choose the best opportunity for you. Then, if you only believed in these two options, you wouldn't be searching for any alternatives because there aren't any alternatives. You would then stay at this job for as long as you think that these are the best two options. Assuming that working in fast food isn't your ultimate goal in life, you would struggle to reach your full potential. There is nothing wrong with working in fast food, but it's not a profession that challenges you to become the best version of yourself, nor does it actually help people but rather causes health problems. Now, you can't judge the person living with this false dichotomy. Some people are taught to think in false dichotomies by their parents, friends, or peer groups simply because they haven't learned about other opportunities yet. They don't know there are other options.

Now, almost everyone knows that there are more employment opportunities than a fast food franchise and a retail store, but the point is that people often live their lives making decisions based on a limited way of thinking. Insert any other job opportunities, goals, or life decisions.

For example, many people believe you have to go to college, or you won't be successful. On its face, this seems harmless enough. Often parents and communities encourage their

THE PROBLEM WITH POTENTIAL

kids to study hard, get good grades, and go to college. But do you *have to* go to college to be successful? Of course not. Steve Jobs didn't go to college, and he was one of the most successful business leaders of all time by founding Apple. Mark Zuckerberg, the founder of Facebook, dropped out of Harvard. Brad Pitt, Ashton Kutcher, and so many more successful people never got a college education and reached massive success. I am not saying I agree with or encourage all of these peoples' life choices. What I am saying is that, per the evidence, college is not the only way to be successful. Therefore, the seemingly helpful and encouraging dichotomy of needing to go to college or you won't be successful isn't true. There are more options. Even among various options like starting a company, sales, acting, and more, college may still be a strong step toward reaching your potential. The point is to start thinking outside of the box to see which option will get you there the fastest based on who you are and where you want to go so you can ultimately reach your potential.

These false dichotomies that you **believe** have been developed within your mind based on your past experiences. Your **past** experiences often shape your present identity. Your present identity determines your **present** actions, which work toward your **future** success. Your future success all starts with what you **believe** is possible. That means that what you believe determines your success. What you believe is often referred to as your identity or worldview. If you identify as a business owner, you have either had a business or are developing one. If you identify as lazy, then you probably act that way. Your **identity,** or set of beliefs about yourself, will determine what decisions you will make in the present and the future. There are negative and positive identities. There are egotistical and untrue identities. The goal is to align your identity with the best version of yourself. For example, you might often think about and speak out loud about your worst mistakes and frustrations rather than recounting your past achievements. When you continually remind yourself of all your failures, you begin to think that you are a failure and become more afraid of failing. Alternatively, whenever you see a difficult challenge, if you recall that you've overcome many other difficult things in the past, you can motivate yourself to overcome the new challenge.

IDENTITY DETERMINES YOUR ACTIONS

Your identity inspires your actions, good or bad, forward or backward. If you see yourself as a person who goes to the gym, it's because you have gone to the gym in the past and it's a regular occurrence in your life. If you don't see yourself as a gym-goer, you probably don't go and aren't developing that habit. Insert any sport, any task, any job, any skill, or any quality, you either believe you are capable of any of these things, or you identify as being incapable. Being capable all starts with the belief that you can accomplish something, following through with action, then starting to make that new habit a part of your identity.

THE PROBLEM WITH POTENTIAL

And this is where a vast majority of people do things backward. The average person doesn't start learning something new if they don't identify as that type of person. I'm not saying you should learn everything. To become a master at something, you must spend more time on that one thing than learning everything else. What I am talking about is following your dreams and taking legitimate steps forward rather than procrastinating. Instead of assuming you aren't able to accomplish things—and therefore never start—start doing the things that your goals require, and you will start believing that you can and will achieve those goals as you begin to build confidence in what you are capable of. These actions will turn into habits, leading to developing your identity to inspire more action. Yet, how can this be so simple?

Similar to the false dichotomy of choice between McDonald's and Walmart jobs, people assume the same false dichotomies about their own identity. Commonly, people believe they are either naturally good at something or naturally bad. And they convince themselves to believe that these are the only two options. They aren't. In fact, every single human being goes through a common identity cycle called the Pygmalion effect starting from when they are little kids to adulthood. When you can see how the Pygmalion effect influences your identity, you can understand how your habits, thoughts, and actions determine your identity. As it turns out, you are more in control of influencing your identity, which leads to confidence, ambitions, and actions, more than you ever realized.

CHAPTER 5: IDENTITY INSPIRES ACTION

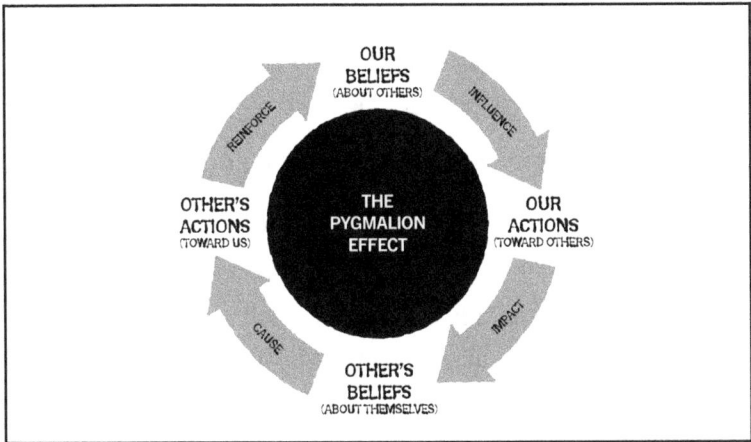

Figure 5.1: The pygmalion effect represents how our external influences impact our internal beliefs.

THE PYGMALION EFFECT

In 1948 famed sociologist Robert K. Merton published a paper on the topic of self-fulfilling prophecies and how a false belief can become true over time because of an invented feedback loop. This is called the Pygmalion effect, which derives its name from the myth of a Greek man who created a female statue and believed it could come to life. Unable to love a human being, he begged the gods to grant his statue life, and Aphrodite, the goddess of love, granted his wish. The Pygmalion effect is similar to that of the placebo effect or imagination effect.[18]

The placebo effect was first discovered in 1799 by a British doctor, John Haygarth. At the time some swindling

---

18 *The Pygmalion Effect: Proving Them Right*. (2021, February 12). Farnam Street. https://tinyurl.com/pygmalionprovingthemright

merchants were claiming that ultra-expensive metal rods called "Perkins tractors" would "draw disease from the body." Knowing this to be completely false, Haygarth made nearly identical rods made of wood but painted to look and feel like metal. He sold them for the same price and found that four out of five patients came back reporting that their pain had been significantly improved. The wood and the metal rods had absolutely no scientific or medicinal benefits. The only benefit they had was from a placebo.

The placebo effect is the idea that if you believe something will help you perform or feel better, it will—even if there is no evidence for the change. In the movie *Harry Potter: The Half-Blood Prince*, Harry pretends to give Ron a magical luck potion called Felix Felicis. Harry acts like he put the potion into Ron's juice, so Ron would think he has become lucky before a quidditch—their version of broomstick soccer—match. Unbeknownst to Ron, Harry faked it and didn't use the potion at all. Ron expected to be lucky and therefore he was confident he would perform well. He went out and performed like a superhuman athlete with luck potion, even though nothing had changed except his expectations. His juice was normal. He was normal. He believed the juice would help him, and therefore he benefited from the placebo effect and had a better outcome. His higher expectations allowed him to achieve something that he previously never thought was possible.

CHAPTER 5: IDENTITY INSPIRES ACTION

The Pygmalion effect is the idea that your actions and the actions of those around you develop your identity, and therefore determine how you act. How you act determines your results, just like Ron, therefore creating a feedback loop around your certain set of beliefs that reinforces your initial set of beliefs. The Pygmalion effect is the official term to describe how high expectations lead to improved performance in a given area and where low expectations lead to worse outcomes, also called the Golem effect.

The Pygmalion effect and the Golem effect explain how you have been conditioned to think your whole life. Once you start to understand why you do what you do, you can start to reshape how you think and feel about yourself and others around you.[19] By developing healthy principles and character traits to overcome the procrastination voices in your head, you will become equipped to overcome the problems that most people avoid in their lives. As discussed earlier in this book, if you avoid your problems, they will inevitably grow to a point where you might think they are too big to be dealt with. But remember, just because you may "**believe**" something is too big to be dealt with doesn't mean that it can't be dealt with. You might just have to look outside the false dichotomies you've convinced yourself exist in order to do so, and that is what this is all about.

---

[19] The Top Essentials. *The Pygmalion Effect/The Rosenthal Experiment*. (2019, October 12). Medium. https://medium.com/@thetopessentials/the-pygmalion-effect-the-rosenthal-experiment-abc3642de889

WHO AM I?

One of the most important questions you will ever ask yourself that will determine your results in life is "Who am I?" The question is often played off with the common phrases of, "I don't know," "I'll figure that out later," or with some regurgitated platitude that you've been told as a kid growing up, but never truly believed about yourself. Struggling with deciding on who you want to become is understandably difficult because deciding your values and who you want to become means you are closing yourself off to other options. In a society that preaches security in having unlimited options, many people get paralyzed by too many choices. There is false security in options because if you never fully commit to doing something, you will perform mediocrely at that activity. Being noncommittal is like joining a baseball team, but instead of doubling down on improving with your team, you are constantly scouting other teams to move to. Therefore, you will practice less with your team and become a more average player who isn't as bought in with the team as you could be. Or it's like getting married but leaving the back door open. If you are not completely committed to marriage, you will likely have a rocky relationship when things get difficult rather than working through some of the hard stuff. Being noncommittal is committing to fail.

To grow, you must be committed to becoming the best version of yourself. Being committed to growth forces you

CHAPTER 5: IDENTITY INSPIRES ACTION

to question if the decisions you make daily are in line with WHO you want to be. It means you can't just make choices based on how you feel at the time, but instead, you make choices that align with who you are striving to be. Making this decision may seem like you are missing out on life by saying no to other options, but in reality, deciding who you want to be will help you discover a well of motivation that is unstoppable. It will help you inspire more action in your life than you thought was possible.

The most interesting lie people perpetuate about themselves from grade school is the following: "I'm not good at math." I bet you've said something like this before, or you've heard it before, and you can interchange math with almost any action or skill. I've said things like this many times, and the reason that saying things like this is self-destructive is that we start believing what we say about ourselves, and then, we start to live it out; therefore, we create a self-fulfilling prophecy.

Similar to the example of reading, imagine that little Johnny is a six-year-old in first grade, learning math for the first time. He had his very first addition test, and unfortunately, his parents were busy, so he didn't get a chance to study, or he simply misunderstood some of the questions. He fails the test. The teacher inadvertently says, "You're not very good at math." Or one of his peers sees his test score, and they say, "You aren't smart at math!" What happens in the young boy's mind? For the very first time in Johnny's short life, he starts to think, "Why is everyone saying that I am bad at math? Maybe I am bad at math…" Johnny is beginning to base his beliefs on what others say about him.

He therefore decides that he is bad at math and every time his parents try to help him get better, he fights them! He believes it's stupid because he feels inferior when he tries math. He has bought into the idea that he was born bad at math. So, he starts to fall behind in his study of math as he spends less and less time developing his skills, and then, another test comes up. Because Johnny didn't study or spend any time developing his math skills, he is nervous and ill-prepared. So, he fails the test yet again. He believed that there was no point in studying because he was inherently bad at math. Johnny grows up and continues to believe and announce to the world that he is not good at math. He has succumbed to the self-fulfilling prophecy of the Golem effect.

Johnny is just a simple example of what many people have done in their minds since childhood. They base their beliefs about their potential on their past mistakes and the opinions of others. Thus, a false narrative is born in one's mind that begins to impact future thoughts and ambitions, which is very similar to the fallacy of proficiency of Chapter 3. Understanding your mentality is everything when it comes to growth.

CHAPTER 5: IDENTITY INSPIRES ACTION

THE PAST DOESN'T DICTATE THE FUTURE

There is a lie perpetuated by society: the past dictates the future. This idea isn't true. The past does NOT dictate the future. The reality is that you have the opportunity to dictate the decisions that shape your future. You decide how you think and feel and will interact with the world around you. Although you can't control every aspect of life, you can control your response to the events that happen to you. If it rains, you can choose to find ways to enjoy the rain. When I was selling books door-to-door in the summer, it wouldn't rain every day, but when it did, it poured. Every year I would be in charge of a certain number of rookies, and I always enjoyed sharing my mentality with them on how I get through rainy days with a great attitude to teach them how to have a positive mindset.

There are two ways to look at rainy days when you are selling. Here are the uncontrollable: Your book bag will get wet. Your feet will be soaked. It will be extremely humid outside. Although this can be miserable, you can improve it by controlling the controllable and finding reasons why rain is great. First, if it's raining, aren't more people in their homes? Meaning you are likely to talk to more people, thus increasing your chances of selling? Also, if it's raining outside and someone opens the door and sees you're a hard-working college student trying to help families with school, aren't they more likely to invite you in because it's raining, and you all

THE PROBLEM WITH POTENTIAL

are getting soaked? Finally, you can wear a rain jacket, bring an umbrella, bring towels, and wear shoes that keep your feet comfortable in the rain, minimizing your discomfort. This mentality led to some of my very best days in sales in some of the worst monsoon conditions I've ever been outside in, and it all started with high expectations and a positive mindset.

You need not feel guilty or angry with yourself over the Pygmalion effect's process growing up because we all start as children with little control over our lives.

Children have very few chances to make decisions, and they don't decide who their parents are. You may have had the best parents, the worst, or somewhere in between, but as adults, you make the decisions for your life. You have a choice. Everything is a choice; how will you make your choices from this moment forward?

CHAPTER 6

OVERCOME THE CYNIC WITHIN

The real trap, however, is self-rejection. As soon as someone accuses me or criticizes me, as soon as I am rejected, left alone, or abandoned, I find myself thinking, "Well, that proves once again that I am a nobody." ... [My dark side says,] I am no good... I deserve to be pushed aside, forgotten, rejected, and abandoned. Self-rejection is the greatest enemy of the spiritual life because it contradicts the sacred voice that calls us the "Beloved." Being the Beloved constitutes the core truth of our existence.

— Henri J.M. Nouwen

THE PROBLEM WITH POTENTIAL

Life truly is what you make of it. You can make a heaven of hell or a hell of heaven. It's all up to you. Living a life where you feel you are in heaven or, oppositely, hell is a journey. It isn't instant. One doesn't think themselves into confidence overnight nor do they think themselves into mediocrity or hypochondria in a mere day. You grow or you stagnate based on your daily mental and physical habits that produce _**action**_. Actions produce habits, which produce thought patterns. Over time you become what you think about. What you think about often becomes a voice in your mind, like your Jiminy Cricket or your shoulder angels. These shoulder angels represent the voice of confidence or the voice of self-doubt. The voice of self-doubt is what I call the cynic within.

What is a cynic? A cynic is a person who believes that there is always a catch or that things can't be that easy or simple. The book definition is a person who believes that people are motivated purely by self-interest. Cynicism isn't in itself a wrong thing, you should have a healthy cynicism for people whom you don't know, your government, and anyone wielding a weapon. In ancient Greece, there was even a school of cynicism started by a man by the name of Antisthenes. He and his followers had a contempt for ease and pleasure. Essentially, cynics struggle to trust others and don't like to make things very easy on themselves. Although cynicism can help keep you safe at times, it also makes you risk-averse and extremely negative.

CHAPTER 6: OVERCOME THE CYNIC WITHIN

In the context of this book, the cynic within describes the little voice in your head that can be further described as the voice of mediocrity. This voice, or thought pattern, tends to rationalize away your motivation to jump out and get started on reaching your goals in life and fulfilling your potential. If left alone, this voice has the **potential** to ***RUIN your life***. This voice has the potential to feed your confidence or to feed your self-doubt. Either way, the voice will continue to talk to you.

Imagine the cynic within as a caricature of an old colleague who lived through your past successes and failures. Still, this particular cynic only looks at your mistakes, and this colleague likes to remind you of them. The cynic within looks for any excuse to hold you back from unlocking your potential. It will take any opportunity to do its best to hold you back through what you **listen** to *and* by what you **SAY**. Some examples of this could be, but are not limited to, TV shows, music, people, self-loathing, and what you say out loud and proud. What you listen to makes your mind think in a certain pattern. When you listen to discouragement, you become discouraged. When you listen to encouragement, you become encouraged. When you listen to a sad song, often you become sad. The same is true of the opposite. Understand that BOTH your outward and your inward influences have a tremendous effect on who you are and who you are becoming.

THE PROBLEM WITH POTENTIAL

EVERYTHING IS CREATED TWICE

The first thing you must understand about overcoming the cynic within is that **everything is created twice.** *Once in your head and once in reality.* Everything you think is the seed to what you will do and ultimately how you feel. You've probably heard the common phrase that **actions speak louder than words**. If you truly believe that everything is created twice, once in your head before you act and once when you act, **then THOUGHTS speak louder than anything**. Your thoughts determine your actions. Your actions determine your habits, which determine your identity. Your identity determines your confidence. Your confidence determines your results. Your results are a product of your thoughts, meaning that your thoughts create limitless potential or a LIMIT to your potential. Your thoughts are potentially life-bringing or life-threatening. Your thoughts dictate who you are, and a large majority of people aren't intentional with their thinking, rather they are "reactionary" to the stimulus around them. This means what you watch on TV, what you listen to on your devices, and who you spend your time with influences your thinking and therefore your potential. This is why your thoughts are extremely important! As a quick reminder, the conversation in your head with yourself and your thoughts is called **self-talk.** Self-talk is what you say to yourself about yourselves AND what you believe about what others say about you. Self-talk, just like any other skill, can be mastered in the same way as shooting a basketball or learning the piano.

CHAPTER 6: OVERCOME THE CYNIC WITHIN

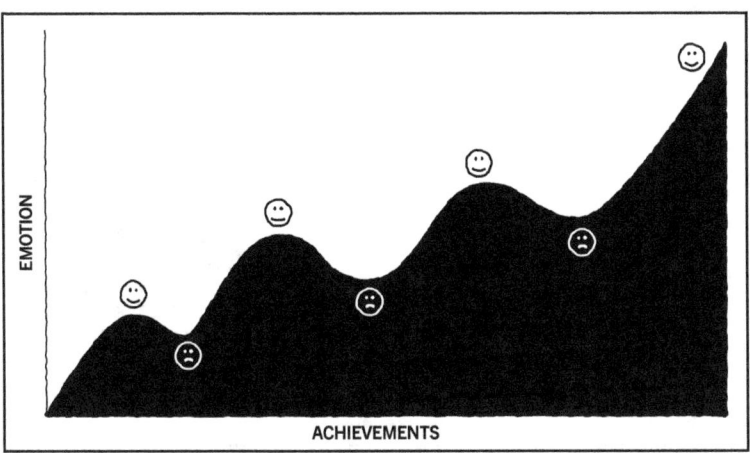

Figure 6.1: Growth isn't linear. You have ups and downs all the time, but you still grow in an upward trajectory over time.

Notice there are TWO distinct parts of the definition. What you say to yourself and what you *believe* about what others say about you. For lack of a better descriptor, self-talk is all in your head. It's the personal conversation between yourself and your shoulder angels. It's your response to your thought patterns.

The conversation goes like this: "Wow, you're not good at this... What's the point in trying?" If you've ever told yourself something like this, you have engaged in negative self-talk. If you've ever told yourself, "I got this! I am unstoppable!" you've experienced positive self-talk. Naturally, positive self-talk encourages you to greater heights while negative self-talk demotivates you to the point of low confidence and limitations. To achieve extraordinary results that match your potential, you must learn to intentionally control your self-talk to encourage you positively without getting ahead of yourself.

THE PROBLEM WITH POTENTIAL

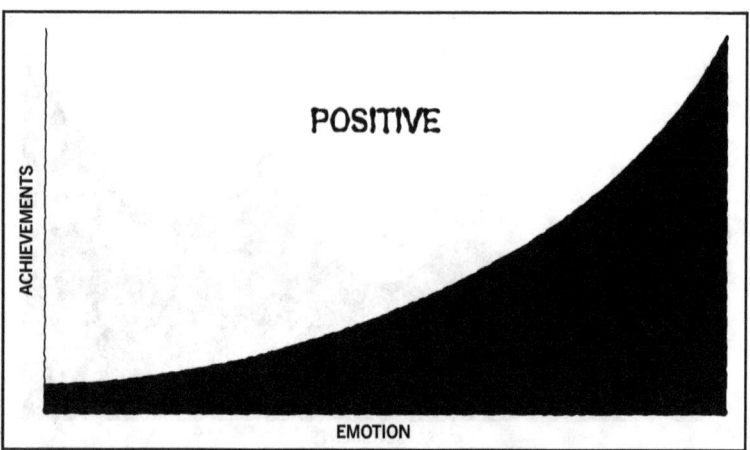

Figure 6.2: This figure represents the positive emotion associated with achievement. The more you achieve, the more confidence you build.

What I mean by this is that you need to use positive self-talk to focus on achieving incremental tasks that build up to a monumental achievement. A big mistake I see many of my ultra-successful business clients make is that they focus too much on the massive results instead of on the small victories. The reason behind this is because of improper expectation management. Improper expectations often create frustration while proper expectations drive you forward. When you get frustrated, you tend to pull back or burn out. I call this a low. When you get excited, you tend to put all your effort into something unsustainably. I call this a high. When you go from high emotions to low emotions, it's like taking a 1,000-foot drop off the top of a roller coaster. You go from being on top of the world to completely down in the dumps. Then, your actions slowly halt until you are excited or motivated again. This is called the *emotional roller coaster*.

CHAPTER 6: OVERCOME THE CYNIC WITHIN

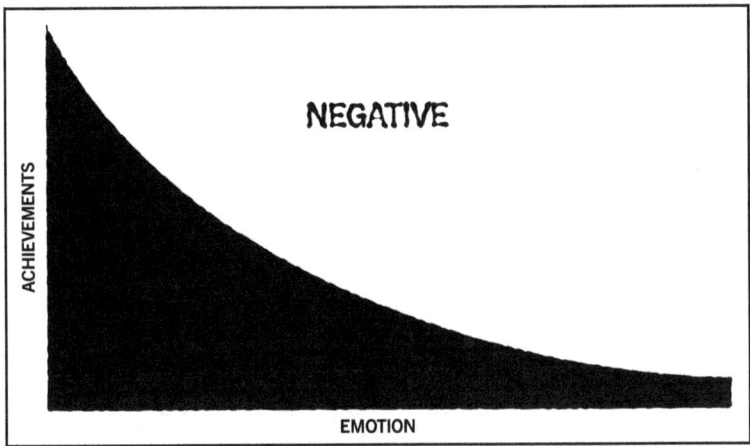

Figure 6.3: This figure represents the negative emotion associated with lack of achievement. The less you achieve, the less confidence you build.

THE EMOTIONAL ROLLERCOASTER

I first heard about the emotional rollercoaster when I was recruiting at Southwestern. My recruiting partners and I would have students learn about our program and be really excited emotionally the first day because of the value you'd gain from participating, just to go home and become nervous at the prospect of no guarantees. And throughout the interview process, their emotions would go up and down and up and down. Only when a student relaxed and looked at all the facts logically did taking on a challenge make sense. Those who went all in because they didn't fall prey to the emotional rollercoaster had great experiences. Those who didn't conquer the rollercoaster felt like they couldn't overcome the challenge and therefore procrastinated taking action towards their

THE PROBLEM WITH POTENTIAL

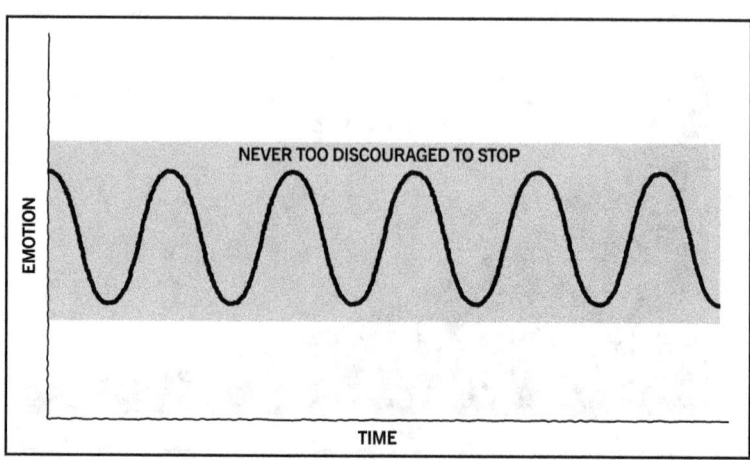

Figure 6.4: This figure represents a healthy emotional consistency pattern.

growth, even though they knew logically the experience would be better than their other options. During the decision process, the emotional roller-coaster was deceiving, causing them to operate without clarity. And this can happen to all of us.

The emotional roller coaster causes *predictable* inconsistency. This is what the cynic within wants. It wants you to be all over the place emotionally, so you can't think or *act* logically. Sometimes, you know you should do something logically, but you don't because of how you feel about it. Logically, you know that emotions are temporary. Still, when you are in the thick of things, you can't think logically and resort to your emotional instincts, predisposing you to avoid challenges. The result of allowing your emotions to dictate your behavior is the following: The only time you get anything done is when you're feeling motivated, and you allow your goals to go on standby every time you hit the next low.

CHAPTER 6: OVERCOME THE CYNIC WITHIN

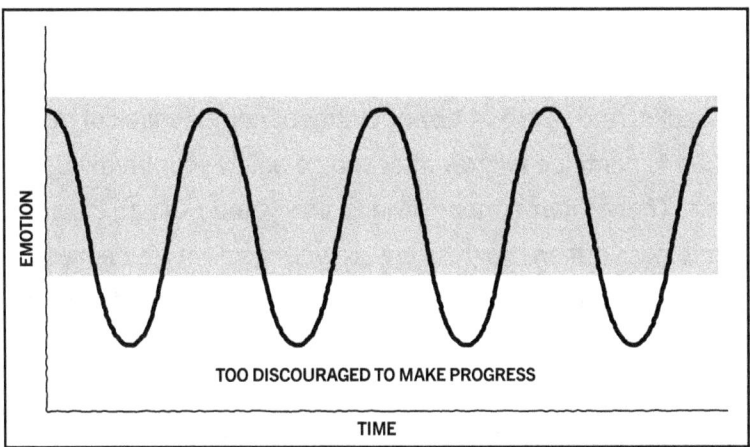

Figure 6.5: This figure represents an unhealthy pattern of emotional consistency.

To reach your potential and consistently grow, it is essential to stay emotionally consistent, not getting too high and not getting too low. You aim to stay in the middle with small dips and valleys in your emotions. You will always have dips and valleys, and emotions themselves aren't a bad thing and are needed in life, but learning to be content with who you are, what you have, and where you are going is a must to reach your potential.

Notice the two different graphics above. In graphic 6.4, you'll notice a healthy emotional consistency pattern. Instead of overreacting negatively or positively to situations, you focus on growing. You celebrate the wins when they happen, and you don't dwell too long on the failures but instead learn and move on to return to normalcy. In graphic 6.5, you'll see an unhealthy pattern of emotional consistency representing the emotional rollercoaster. This graphic shows intense excitement at good results and progress, followed by a plummet back to earth and down to disappointment when you experience failures or setbacks. And with that disappointment comes a lack of motivation to continue to grow after you go below your breaking point. These intense mood swings slow you down and cause you to miss out on progress toward your goals in life because you never have a sense of normalcy. If you aren't excited or in the mood, you are less motivated; if you are incredibly disappointed, you don't want to take action. Often, those who reach their potential aren't more special than others, but instead, they regulate their emotions and catch themselves when they are negative, celebrate the wins when they can, and don't overreact to what's going on. They just stay focused on the process of progress and mastering the cynic within instead of worrying about the results. They just take consistent action; to do that, you must conquer the cynic within that wants you to ride the emotional rollercoaster.

MASTERING THE CYNIC WITHIN

To start mastering *your* cynic within, and thus create a less intense emotional roller coaster and a better growth curve trajectory, you need to start to monitor and change all the little self-talk conversations you have with yourself.

Self-talk is rarely taught in school in a personalized or practical way, so the average person likely hasn't learned the concept, technique, and power of positive self-talk yet. This means the average person has been perpetually flying blind in this area of expertise with their minds likely being

CHAPTER 6: OVERCOME THE CYNIC WITHIN

their biggest enemy. To do this, you must accept that the past doesn't dictate the future. This is easier said than done because your past life experiences have programmed you to **think** and **believe** in a perspective of how the world works, but this perspective is often faulty.

In fact, according to the National Library of Medicine, you remember *NEGATIVE* experiences much clearer than positive experiences. Why? Because your brain wants you to live. In moments of failure or fear, when you have negative experiences, you experience PAIN. This means there is a very good chance that you think negatively more consistently than positively. Embarrassment is usually more intense than laughter and will be remembered longer. And then, the past starts to dictate your future decisions, which is the opposite of what will help you be successful.[20]

When you experience pain or intense emotion, your brain remembers this event more clearly to avoid this pain. That is just how your brain works when you don't focus on wiring your brain in a way that will help you be successful. The cynic tries to tell you to avoid *all* pain. But not every pain you experience is bad pain. For example, it may hurt to run two miles based on the fact that you feel tired and sore, but in the grand scheme of things your body gets healthier through this pain. So, what you need to start considering with your self-talk is what is bad pain that should be avoided and what is good pain that you should rewire your brain to get excited about?! Applicably, you must start actively producing healthy

---

20 Rehman, I. *Classical Conditioning*. (2022, August 22). National Library of Medicine. https://www.ncbi.nlm.nih.gov/books/NBK470326/

self-talk in place of negative self-talk. Below are the four types of self-talk and a simple exercise to get you started. Before we jump into that, I just want to say that I attribute all I know about self-talk from the sales managers who mentored me and taught this when I worked at Southwestern Advantage. I am eternally grateful for this knowledge that I was taught when I was a sales manager at the company.

THE FOUR TYPES OF SELF-TALK

The first type of self-talk is called *Negative Perspective Self-Talk*. This type of self-talk is self-harming in nature. It's when you accept negative perspectives about yourself and internally process them to become part of your identity. Many phrases of this type of self-talk can sound like the following: "I'm stupid." "I'm not pretty enough." "He is more muscular than me." "I can't measure up." "No one likes me." "I suck at soccer." Clearly, this type of self-talk is harmful, and what is most unfortunate is that this type of self-talk is the MOST COMMON type of self-talk.

The second type of self-talk I call the *Realization Self-Talk*. This type of self-talk promotes procrastination, but it is at least less harmful than the first type of self-talk. This type of self-talk happens when you realize you need to change something about yourself, but you are intentionally or unintentionally putting it off. It includes phrases like, "I should…" "I would…" "I need to…" etc. You've realized you need to change, and you see the negative effects of your habits, but you just haven't **decided** to change yet.

CHAPTER 6: OVERCOME THE CYNIC WITHIN

The third type of self-talk I call *Affirmative Self-Talk*. This type of self-talk is finally in the healthy category! It is identity-based in nature, and it builds you up by relying on truth statements you believe about yourself. For example, "I am strong." "I am unstoppable." "I am clean." "I am organized" "I am good at basketball." etc. This is a wonderful starting point. These affirmations remind you of your state of being and who you are regardless of your external circumstances.

Number four: *Decision to Change Self-Talk*. This type of self-talk is the BEST and most life-giving self-talk you can do. It is action-based in nature, and it is used in the state of BEING phraseology. This self-talk follows an internal decision to change your actions. You are not maintaining the status quo, like with *Affirmative Self-Talk*; you have decided to make changes to grow into a better version of yourself. This self-talk requires action and is more focused on who you will someday be if you make good choices and actions to develop yourself into the best version of yourself. For example: "I am a person of purpose and every single thing that I do, I do with intentionality for the bigger picture." "I am an organized person, and every single day, I am improving in this area to release stress in my life." "I am becoming the best version of myself every day because I am giving my best effort to improve."

PERCEPTION IS NOT REALITY

I'm sure you have probably heard that your perception is often your reality. Well, in truth reality is reality, and perception is a subjective lens you look through based on what you

THE PROBLEM WITH POTENTIAL

know and what you don't know. In other words, perception is your best guess on what reality looks like based on your current knowledge. For example, everyone thought the world was flat centuries ago. At the time, the overwhelming majority perception of people was that earth was the center of the universe. Until Ferdinand Magellan's trip around the globe in the early 1500s, people just thought you could fall off the edge of the world if you sailed too far in one direction. Today, we know the globe is spherical. For all the people who lived before that time who believed the world was flat, it didn't make the world flat, it just influenced their perception, which opened up a doorway to intense fear that limited their global exploration to what was comfortable. It was only when Magellan decided to break the norm that allowed for the fear of falling off Earth's edge to disappear. The same is true with the negative beliefs in one's mind.

Even if you have believed something so strongly and have perceived it for so long, what you think about yourself may not be reality. So, how do you know what is reality and what isn't?

Have you ever heard of a fixed versus growth mindset? Sally grows up and is taught that conquering new challenges is exciting! New challenges are difficult, and they require problem-solving and creativity. Although learning something new or overcoming a challenge is difficult up front, the reward of finding a solution feels so much better than the initial feeling of frustration! Sally always finishes what she starts; as a result, and over time, she believes that she can conquer any problem that comes her way. She is confident in her critical-thinking skills.

CHAPTER 6: OVERCOME THE CYNIC WITHIN

On the other hand, Shelly is taught growing up that sometimes things are just too hard for some people. She is told that she either has natural-born talent or she doesn't. She can't develop skills or mental processes to overcome new challenges; instead, she can only do things that she is good at naturally. That way, she won't get frustrated or look foolish failing at something in front of the masses. She should stay safe and live in her comfort zone, and all will be okay. If it's too hard, she can just find something else and stick with that.

We generally flip back and forth between these two mindsets based on our situation, or where we find ourselves on the emotional roller coaster. If we are down in the dumps at the bottom of our roller coaster, we will probably think in the fixed mindset. While at the top, we are more often thinking in the growth mindset. It is rare to find someone who is fully growth-minded or fixed-minded. Our mindset is constantly shifting and changing based on our daily mental choices through self-talk and our daily actions, which are our habits.

SELF-TALK EXERCISE

Now, for the exercise. I want you to write down everything you've said to yourself from the *Negative Perspective Self-Talk* and *Realization Self-Talk* categories from the past week, day, or hour on a piece of paper. Take your time to just write it out. If you are being honest with yourself, you may have a pretty long list of these categories from just the past few hours. I want you to know that these are all lies that you are telling yourself because you have not yet learned the habit of positive personal self-talk. You will learn that now.

I want you to pick your personal top two most troublesome self-talk examples and I want you to cross them out and rewrite them in the *Decision to Change Self-Talk* style. For example: "I'm not smart enough," could morph into, "I am capable of any intellectual problem because I always do whatever it takes to understand something. Regardless of how confusing things may seem at first, I always give my best effort to understand them until I master the concepts." Do this with those top two negative self-talk phrases. How does it feel?

This is a great exercise to do once, but it's even better to make these affirmations a consistent part of your monthly, weekly, or even daily routine. For the first six years of learning to manage and train my mind to think more positively so I could stay more emotionally consistent, I would journal nearly every single evening about how I was feeling. I would pick five affirmations and write them out. I would recall three victories from my work for the day. I would choose one thing I wanted to focus on tomorrow, and I would finish with a paragraph to vent and let out my thoughts and frustrations so I could let them go. This helped me to sell over $200,000 worth of educational books while managing a million-dollar business of over twenty-five salespeople when I was just twenty-three years old.

Doing things like this once is helpful, but intentionally making good habits like this common is difficult. Herein lies the problem with potential that is most prevalent with us all. Unintentional actions are due to our subconscious habits.

CHAPTER 7

THE SUBCONSCIOUS POWER OF HABITS

Habits either empower you with the strength needed to lead your life where you want to go or make you feel like you have no control.

Starting a new habit is the easy part. You are on an emotional high because you are excited to get the end result. The hard part is continuing to perform the same or similar tasks even when you don't want to. The art of discipline is following through when no one else is looking, even when you would rather do anything else.

In the book *The Power of Habit*, there is a great story about a man who had a bad car accident and a brain injury. This individual would suffer from short-term memory loss for the rest of his life. *Before* this tragic accident, he had lived in a community with a pond nearby that he used to walk around every single morning, and most surprisingly, *after* the accident, he would continue to do the same. Oddly enough he would commonly find himself walking around the path without any idea of how he got there as he didn't even remember starting the walk. His old habits from *before* the car accident stuck with him regardless of his short-term memory loss and damage to his brain.[21] As it turns out, your habits are stored in a separate part of your brain from where short-term memory is stored. While short-term memory requires constant focus and effort to retain, your habits continue to work behind the scenes entirely *subconsciously*.

When your brain develops a habit, it is trying to help you by creating mental shortcuts to allow you to think about more pressing matters that aren't routine which is accomplished by the brain carving out neuro pathways through repeated action. By doing so, your habits become ingrained in your brain, allowing you to automate your routine actions and focus on complex problem solving. Sometimes the best part of having a habit is the resulting cue or reminder that causes you to act.

For example, think about when you brush your teeth. There are a couple of ingrained habits that you may not realize you have. For example, right before bed, your mouth might feel or taste bad around the same time you need to brush your teeth, causing you to brush your teeth. While the habit could

---

[21] Duhigg, C. (2012). *The Power of Habit: Why We Do What We Do in Life and Business*. Random House.

CHAPTER 7: THE SUBCONSCIOUS POWER OF HABITS

feel like a chore, the specific movements you make with the brush are likely in a pattern that you repeat almost every single time you brush your teeth. You don't even need to think about how you are brushing because it is something you've done for years. In the event you fail to brush your teeth, you might struggle to sleep or have bad-tasting breath as a result of neglecting this habit. It's like sleeping in for the first time in months and waking up feeling groggier than you normally do because your body isn't used to waking at that later time.

Sometimes you repeat habits that you don't even realize you are doing, like biting your nails, eating junk food at a certain time at night, or going to the gym at the same time every day. With that being said, habits are neither good nor evil; they are only what you make of them. Some habits, such as smoking, will take you to an early grave, while others, such as exercise, will extend your life. No matter what habits you have already formed, your habits are *powerful*, and they are *subconscious*.

Habits are often developed unintentionally—whether you like it or not—because your brain associates positive feelings with those habits. The solution is understanding how to start building a foundation of strong habits that put you in a place to win, and then intentionally implementing small, incremental improvements over time.

In modern culture, there is a general lack of education on habits. There is no class that dives into the complexities of the brain and how to develop better habits for your life. Unless your parents or a connection teaches you about habits, you

THE PROBLEM WITH POTENTIAL

have to seek out the information on your own. The issue is that you have to know that you need to learn about habits to start searching for the information! At the same time, you are conditioned to want to be comfortable from media advertisements, social media, movie stars, and so forth. Add this constant subliminal messaging of comfort to the fact that your brain is designed to avoid pain, and you have a serious concoction of influences that encourage you to develop comfortable habits. Unfortunately, what's comfortable doesn't lead to accomplishing your dreams or helping those around you. *Constant comfort leads to complacency.*

As you become more comfortable, your habits become those of avoidance of pain, and you begin to make decisions based on comfort in a part of your brain that isn't even conscious of you. Habits are stored in a subconscious part of your brain called the basal ganglia, meaning that your habits are so *subconsciously powerful* that you don't even notice them. Meaning, you avoid hard things without even realizing it! This is where being unintentional can become detrimental to your potential. I don't mention this fact to discourage you in your pursuit of reaching your true potential, rather I believe that with this knowledge comes the power for you to intentionally wire your brain to seek out challenges and build habits that *help* you rather than *hinder* you.

In pursuit of great achievement, you must take habits seriously. It takes a minimum of twenty-one days to build a habit. To break a habit, it takes a minimum of eighteen days, and it can take as long as 254 days to break a really old

CHAPTER 7: THE SUBCONSCIOUS POWER OF HABITS

habit.[22] If you can focus on developing good habits for ninety days, you'll probably never stop making that habit, as it will be ingrained in your brain as you live your life. It will become a part of your lifestyle and identity.

PAVLOV'S CLASSICAL CONDITIONING

In 1897, a Russian scientist, Ivan Pavlov, conducted a study on the response dogs make to being fed. He hypothesized that dogs would salivate when the food was right in front of them due to the sight and smell of the food. Not only did the dogs salivate when the food was in front of them, but they also learned to salivate when they heard the footsteps of the man who was bringing the food to the dogs before they even saw it. The dogs learned to involuntarily respond to the events leading up to being fed. What he discovered is now called classical conditioning.[23]

Classical conditioning is the process in which an automatic response occurs due to a specific occurrence or stimulus. We have the exact same responses with our habits and conditioning.[24]

---

22 Author interview. (2012, March 5). *Habits: How They Form and How to Break Them*. Fresh Air, NPR. https://www.npr.org/2012/03/05/147192599/habits-how-they-form-and-how-to-break-them

23 Rehman, I. *Classical Conditioning*. (2022, August 22). National Library of Medicine. https://www.ncbi.nlm.nih.gov/books/NBK470326/

24 Manoylov, M., & Mendez, M. *How Long Does it Take to Break a Habit? 5 Science-Backed Tips to Change Unhealthy Habits*. (2022, May 26). Insider. https://www.insider.com/guides/health/mental-health/how-long-does-it-take-to-break-a-habit

THE PROBLEM WITH POTENTIAL

For example, when you haven't gone on vacation in a long time but then you take a trip with no work, at first you may feel weird or out of place with the initial traveling experience. You might feel like you should be working or doing something productive with that time instead. Even though you would know that you don't need to do any work, there could be a bit of an itch to work because it's what you are used to. You have been classically conditioned to work without breaks, and your mind and body are reacting to your normal routine like that of Pavlov's experiment.

Many people struggle with relaxing on vacations because they have developed the habit of always working. It is easy for your work ethic habits to take over even when you are intentionally trying to relax! That's the power of our habits.

Almost no one can take a vacation for ninety days, but that's not the point. The point is that you have these deep-seated habits hardwired in your brain—some are good, and some are not. So, why does this matter? Well, as incredible as it is to tackle your self-talk and rewrite your negative beliefs as positive ones once, you won't see a big difference in your life holistically if you only act once. It won't make a *world-changing* difference in your life to become suddenly motivated and read 200 pages of a book on any one given day, then never do it again and allow the book to sit, unfinished, while collecting dust. You likely won't recall any information either because you don't store long-term memory or build habits through doing something once. That is like going to the gym once a year for ten hours and expecting to be healthy and fit for the rest of the year. Achievement doesn't

CHAPTER 7: THE SUBCONSCIOUS POWER OF HABITS

just happen overnight; it comes from consistent efforts over a long period of time. But if you can build a habit for ninety days without stopping, you can build a lifestyle that will last the rest of your life. It takes twenty-one days to build a habit and eighteen to break a habit. So, once you've built it, it's harder to break it. The difficult bit is being disciplined and intentional *long enough* to build the habit you want to see in your life. Consistency begins with inconsistency, so when you start, be prepared to struggle. It's all worth it in the end.

START SMALL

To do this, you need to start being intentional with your daily routines and *start small* by implementing *sustainable habits*. Pick *one thing* that you will be able to consistently do every single day, *no matter what*. For example, wake up at your very first alarm and don't hit snooze. Don't play on your phone or scroll social media for an hour before bed. Go to the gym or exercise for at least twenty minutes every day. Cut out processed sugar from soda or sweets from your diet and replace it with fresh fruit. Drink a full glass of water the first thing you do in the morning. Regardless of what habit you choose for yourself, all of these options will add value to your life and help you feel more energized, and they are *simple*.

Do a simple habit for three weeks, then add *one* crucial habit to your list. If you struggle to maintain your new habits, go at your own pace. If it takes a bit longer to build that first habit before a strong crucial habit, stay focused on that first one until you've

THE PROBLEM WITH POTENTIAL

mastered it before adding more habits. Success in this area of life is more about identifying the biggest habits that are holding you back and prioritizing the major good habits you need to reach your potential. Don't get bogged down in trying to accomplish everything at once. Realize that even the seemingly small wins build up over time. If you try to add too many things all at once, your brain may freak out and you will feel the urge to quit as you struggle to keep up with all you are trying to accomplish. Take one step at a time and focus on the small wins.

After a few months, you will have successfully built some incredible habits that are helping you become who you want to be. If you want to take this to the next level, schedule a time for a weekly "habits reflection" on the same day of every week for an hour to kick off your week with momentum. On that day, think about your self-talk and habits for the week. Write down what habits are helping you and what habits are hindering you. Focus on eliminating all distractions when you do this and, based on your answers, choose to make one or two changes each week to help yourself build habits in the direction of where you want to go.

When you hit a snag in motivation, remember that it will get **easier** over time as your body and mind start to incorporate the action into your subconscious mind by creating a new habit.

CHAPTER 8

THE PAIN PARADOX

You can't avoid pain in life.
The only choice you have is the timing of the pain.
Now, or later.

For the longest time, there has been a debate over whether one's IQ level will determine the outcome of one's life. Is success predetermined from birth? In the book *Outliers* by Malcolm Gladwell, Gladwell shares the story of the Beatles' musical success. John Lennon, Paul McCartney, George Harrison, and Ringo Starr made up one of the most famous bands of all time, accruing over twenty number-one hits over eight years as a band. Most modern Americans know all about how famous the Beatles were, but most people don't know about how the Beatles got their start.

THE PROBLEM WITH POTENTIAL

The Beatles began their ascent to being one of the best bands of all time by taking a huge risk. They all left their jobs and schools behind to start working as a bar band in the red-light district of Hamburg, Germany. Not the most prestigious gig to start with, you might think. They started as an unrehearsed band, as they hadn't played together before. All of the members had very little stage experience. But the Beatles knew that this was their chance, so they emphatically started playing for sets that lasted as long as **six hours**. Not only did they play for extremely long periods of time late into the evenings, but they also did it **six days per week**.[25] That's a lot of music, singing, and standing on stage.

No wonder the Beatles created so many incredible songs. They played so much that music became a part of them. They put in their time early on to develop into incredible musicians through hours and hours of practice, and when they were finally discovered, their investment of time paid off for the rest of their lives. They understood that the short-term pain of playing six days per week with six-hour sets made them better at their craft.

 No matter who you are, that is a grueling schedule even if it's something you enjoy doing. Singing for six hours would make me and many others completely hoarse. Playing the guitar for six hours would leave most hands bleeding, especially at first.

---

25 Admin. *60 Years Since the Beatles Started their Professional Career*. (2020, August 17). The Daily Beatle. http://webgrafikk.com/blog/news/60-years-since-the-beatles-started-their-professional-career/

CHAPTER 8: THE PAIN PARADOX

The stage lights would make you sweat, and you wouldn't have much time to take a break. You are playing regardless of how you feel. By the end of the performance, you would be exhausted just to have to do it again and again for weeks upon weeks in a row.

At the beginning of the Beatles' career, they weren't well known, they didn't make a lot of money, and they worked themselves as hard as possible in an undesirable district in Hamburg. But they had a dream of being successful musicians. They loved music. They would go through whatever pain it took to be successful. Because of their early discipline to continue working hard through the unfavorable conditions for years, they became one of the most successful and influential bands of all time. The Beatles got through the initial pain and developed incredible skills, then the rest of their musical career was a success. They bought in, like so many others in various fields, to the pain paradox.

The pain paradox is the idea that human beings naturally avoid as much pain as possible assuming that a good life is a life without pain, but having a good life requires pain. The pain paradox doesn't necessarily deal with physical or circumstantial pain as much as it deals with how you react to those circumstances, and when you choose to experience growing pains that lead to success. In the concept of the pain paradox, no matter how much you try to avoid pain, you will experience pain in your life whether in the short-term (through growing pains) or in the long-term (via consequences).

THE PROBLEM WITH POTENTIAL

Some pain is controllable, and other pain is uncontrollable or circumstantial. Uncontrollable pain is associated with uncontrollable circumstances, such as rain while you are working outside, if a tree falls on your house, or getting robbed or mugged. It also can include how you grew up and anything else you had little choice over. Controllable pain is synonymous with growing pains. They are pains that you have a choice about when you experience them. Growing pains can include but aren't limited to facing rejection, learning through failure, being mocked or made fun of, physical exercise, etc. To reach your potential, you must suffer through these growing pains. If you avoid them, you could miss out on many significant parts of life.

For the controllable part of pain, you can choose when that pain occurs in your life. You can control when you experience growing pains based on your intentional effort to grow as a person. As you grow, the pain becomes more manageable, and you learn to control your emotions when mistakes arise.

Pain is a response the brain sends to the conscious mind when something is wrong or damaged. No one *likes* pain, so the natural inclination is to avoid pain at all costs. But to live life to your greatest potential, you will have to go through growing pains. You may not be able to avoid pain—this is out of your control—but you can choose to deal with pain on your own terms. This means you decide the timing in your life when you experience controllable growing pains.

CHAPTER 8: THE PAIN PARADOX

NOW OR LATER?

To further illustrate this point, imagine that everyone has a pile of heavy boulders that they have to move from one hill to another. You can choose to move all the boulders before breakfast every morning for your entire life or you can front-load the movement of the boulders to one intense portion of your life and never have to move the boulders again for the rest of your life. Which would you choose?

The idea of the pain paradox helps you understand that if you can deal with the pain of your problems as directly as possible in life you will have more success and an easier, more productive life later on. Thus, the struggle between discipline and short-term pleasure is born.

Short-term pain is not fun. Short-term pain sounds miserable unless... is there less pain overall later? Short-term pleasure almost always sounds fantastic! But short-term pleasure can come at a cost. There is a false dichotomy that you have to choose pain or pleasure. Have you noticed that earning something after you've worked hard to get it, actually feels better overall? Short-term pleasure is best experienced and enjoyed as a reward for discipline. If you allow yourself to overindulge in short-term pleasures, you risk becoming habitually accustomed to doing things that feel good but aren't good for you in the long-term.

THE PROBLEM WITH POTENTIAL

One of my favorite children's movies illustrates this point brilliantly. *Wall-E* is a movie about a couple of robots, Wall-E and EVE, that fall in love while trying to transport the last living plant from the Earth to the human race aboard a technologically advanced spaceship. Once Wall-E and EVE get to the spaceship, they see humans for the first time. In this dystopian children's movie, the humans have become extremely overweight, and weak in stature, and their minds have become numb from the oversaturation of media, videos, and fast food. In avoiding physical pain, eating healthy, working out, and stretching one's mind to learn, these humans have put off their pain for years, culminating in medical issues, lethargic behaviors, and low achievements.

SHORT-TERM PAIN VERSUS SHORT-TERM PLEASURE

The lesson is that pleasure to the extreme will eventually limit your confidence and momentum in life. Short-term pain yields long-term benefits. So, the choice is this: short-term pleasure, which leads to long-term pain, or short-term pain, which leads to long-term pleasure? This short-term pain is what we call discipline. Discipline is doing what you want **most**, not what you want **now**. Meaning that in the moment, you may put off your short-term desires to take steps towards your long-term desires.

CHAPTER 8: THE PAIN PARADOX

When I was in my early twenties selling books door-to-door, my year would look something like this: From January to May, I would work sixty to seventy hours per week recruiting at college campuses. In the summers I would work between eighty to ninety hours per week depending on my leadership position. In the fall, I would take three months off and work ten to fifteen hours a week and have several vacations lined up. I would have a couple of work meetings in various parts of the country, but these were often relaxed and educational. I would have nearly all of December off for family and friends and the Christmas holiday season. I did this schedule for seven years. I made friends, pushed myself, and grew immensely. By the time I was twenty-four years old, I owned two houses, had no debt, was in the top 1% of income earners for my age, and I had influenced hundreds of young people to believe in themselves that they could do whatever they put their mind to. More importantly, I had met and was married to a beautiful wife who loved me for who I am. I didn't have super fun, vacation-driven, and video-game-filled summers as I did in high school, but I maximized my time. This set me up with an incredible foundation in life. By twenty-four, I didn't have to work for anyone else if I didn't want to. I didn't have to worry as much about money or retirement. I had developed incredibly rare and valuable skills to start a business from scratch anywhere in the country, and I could replicate it with other companies. I had a massive business network of alumni from where I worked. The list goes on for what I am thankful for.

THE PROBLEM WITH POTENTIAL

To make this happen, to achieve what I wanted, I didn't spend much of college partying, although I did have fun as a reward for my hard work. I didn't work an easy job, and I didn't try to fit in. I made sacrifices by not taking summer vacations with the family. I put all of this off, and now I do all those things while my peers and others seem constantly frustrated at work. I am not unique and don't want a free pass. Discipline spent now earns you freedom and options later. For me, it all started by knocking on the first door of my sales career, being terrible at sales, and being rejected over 3,500 times my first summer when I was eighteen. I was simply making the difficult decision to be disciplined enough to go to the next door, which has made all the difference. Most importantly, I thank God for the results, for without faith in my creator, I would have never had the strength to do so without Him and some incredible mentors and friends in my life.

I don't believe that I have *made it*. And I don't think I am that special or innately talented. Instead, I am still learning and growing. I will never "arrive," as growth is a never-ending process. I have big plans and a lot of discipline developed to achieve them. What I no longer have to struggle with is the typical limitations of time and money to pursue what I truly love doing: Inspiring others to believe in themselves, think big, bridge their knowledge gaps, and do what inspires them so they can add value to the people around them. Together, we can make the world a better place.

CHAPTER 8: THE PAIN PARADOX

If you can learn to be disciplined in spurts long enough for good habits to form, you can accomplish much more in your life. You'll be surprised to see that the world gets out of your way if you know what you want and are willing to work.

Naturally, most people can logically buy into the idea of a better long-term gain and would give up some pleasures now for less pain. You can often agree with this, then slide right back into avoiding hard things. If the way to a better future is to be disciplined and do the hard things now, why is reaching dreams and goals still so uncommon?

The answer is complex, but one thing is sure: you often perform to the commonly accepted expectations of your peers, mentors, and most importantly, your close friends and your personal perception of your self-worth and abilities.

CHAPTER 9

THE HIERARCHY OF FRIENDSHIPS

Friends can be your limit or push your limit higher.

I remember returning to college after my first summer selling books as a sophomore during the fall semester of 2016. I moved into a six-bedroom apartment with four other guys splitting the rent with me. I had met these guys on my dorm room floor as a freshman, and I liked them as friends, so during the prior semester, we had all signed leases for the year. I was excited to spend time with the guys, and we had a lot of fun when we returned from the break.

At the time, I didn't expect how much the people I surrounded myself with would impact my behavior and thought patterns.

THE PROBLEM WITH POTENTIAL

Before moving in, I had surrounded myself with some incredibly motivated entrepreneurs with whom I sold books, which really made a massive difference in my personal confidence and success during the summer. As I mentioned, we would wake up and focus for countless hours a week, and we'd even learned to enjoy the discomfort of rejection because we knew we were growing. I lived with one of these booksellers, and he and I were on a great gym schedule every morning. Working out together and holding each other accountable was much easier than trying to do everything alone. He had a great impact on me, and he and I went on to build a healthy routine that year.

On the other hand, my other roommates really liked to party. I'm not saying you should never celebrate, but there is a line between celebration and overindulgence, at the time, I chose to get sucked into that culture to medicate some of my struggles in building long-term solid relationships. Hence, my internal problems began to limit my potential. As a result, my focus shifted from "How can I grow the most so I can help the most people?" to "How can I fit in and enjoy myself the most?" I allowed my external influences to distract me from what mattered most: helping others.

For nearly three months, I focused entirely on those friends and how I could overindulge in the party culture, and I focused less and less on maximizing my time. I was still a good student, and I had other things going on, but my "free

CHAPTER 9: THE HIERARCHY OF FRIENDSHIPS

time" was utilized on many timewasters. I continued to do this until I started spending more time with my managers from Southwestern. These incredible people were motivated to make things happen and change the world. Just by literally being around them, I felt more motivated to achieve my goals. And when they helped me learn to be a leader, they encouraged me to focus on helping more and more people and have a tangible impact on their lives. It was then, as a teenager, that I really saw the massive influence that your friends can have on your future. They can either distract you or encourage you. And while you can always fight the urge to follow your friends, sometimes it's best just to find new friends with similar goals so you can do what inspires you, like my roommate who would always go to the gym with me.

YOUR FRIENDS INFLUENCE YOUR MENTALITY

Who you are becoming has as much to do with your mentality as it has to do with **who** you spend your time with. Not all friends are equal; some pull you down, others lift you up, others encourage complacency, while others push you to be your best. Your thoughts form your identity, and the people you spend time with influence your thoughts. That means that with intentionality, you can become a better version of yourself by changing your habits and finding good friends. So, you need to look at who you spend your time with and monitor

THE PROBLEM WITH POTENTIAL

how they impact your internal thoughts about yourself and start removing any negative influences upon your growth. You need to start looking for like-minded people who inspire you to become the best version of yourself. Sometimes, that means going to networking groups, finding a new church, mingling with a new group of people at work, or just being more intentional with your healthy relationships. Regardless of where you find them, your group of people is out there. And they either have similar goals or have accomplished them already and will inspire you to get where you are trying to go.

As you focus on spending time with inspiring friends, you start spending more time with like-minded people who appreciate your pursuit of growth, and you start spending less time with negative influences. Although you may spend less time with some past negative influences, like my former college roommates, don't feel like you are "missing out" because growing to help others is more important than pleasing everyone.

Whether you are looking for new friends to replace some negative influences or to spend more time with your positive friends, be prepared for a slow transition period where your mentality shifts into a more positive direction. The friends you spend time with will help you bolster your identity in the direction you intentionally want to go and reflect your valuable strengths rather than weaknesses, just like when incredible Southwestern salespeople surrounded me. I'm not saying that you should look for a bunch of people who agree with

CHAPTER 9: THE HIERARCHY OF FRIENDSHIPS

everything that you agree with, but rather, find people who challenge you to be your best, believe in your capabilities, call you out when you are complacent and want to see you succeed for no other reason because they care about you.

SPILLOVER EFFECT

Remember when we discussed self-talk? As a reminder, self-talk is what you say to yourself about yourself and what you believe in what others say about you. The second part of self-talk has very little to do with your internal thoughts and everything to do with who you surround yourself with. Who you surround yourself with has the power to build you up or tear you down. If you are intentional with whom you decide to spend your time, you will unlock potential like you never thought possible. Not only will you have less opposition thrown your way, but you will also have incredible new ideas and inspiration come up in conversation to challenge you to grow.

When you surround yourself with people who challenge you to be the best version of yourself and see a positive change in your results at your job or in life, it is known as the *spillover effect*. According to researchers at the Kellogg School of Management at Northwestern University, if you sit within a twenty-five-foot radius of a high performer, your performance will increase by an average of 15%. The Kellogg School of Management estimated a million-dollar increase in overall yearly profit due to the high performer's positive spillover to the technology company's staff.

THE PROBLEM WITH POTENTIAL

Unfortunately, the same is true for sitting next to a toxic or low performer, but the impact is more severe. Researchers found that if you sat within a twenty-five-foot radius of these performers, your performance could decrease by nearly 30%! They found that while it often takes a month for the effects of the positive spillover to occur, the harmful effects of the toxic spillover were *immediate* and often reached further than twenty-five yards. Who you spend your time around truly matters. In the context of your life and career, you need to stop spending time with toxic performers and start spending time with superstars.[26]

One of countless examples of the spillover effect occurred to me when I was in my early twenties and spent some time with friends who were ten to fifteen years my senior. I remember hearing about what they would do professionally and how they would live. Once, on the beach in Florida, I was sitting by the pool with a friend who told me about his successful Airbnb business that netted him a bunch of extra cash each year with little to no effort after getting set up. I was around twenty-two years old, and I had never seriously thought about owning short-term or long-term rentals, but it was logical for him, and he was successful at it. From that conversation, he inspired me to invest in a short-term rental, and now I have a cash-flowing property just like my friend, thanks to the spillover effect.

---

[26] Stone, E. *Sitting Near a High-Performer Can Make You Better at Your Job.* (2019, May 10). Kellogg Insight. https://insight.kellogg.northwestern.edu/article/sitting-near-a-high-performer-can-make-you-better-at-your-job

CHAPTER 9: THE HIERARCHY OF FRIENDSHIPS

Another friend told me about how his wife did some sweepstaking. Sweepstaking, in this case, is where you find big corporate company commercial contests and submit professionally done videos for a chance to win a large cash prize. She did exceptionally well. In fact, during my senior year in college, one of my roommates ended up being on one of the commercials and was paid $10,000 to be in just that one commercial that happened to win! Could you even imagine? Until now, I had never realized that you could make money doing something other than working a job or owning a small business. There are so many more opportunities than the norm!

Furthermore, because I got involved in selling books door-to-door early in my college career, I met some incredible friends who were master salespeople and recruiters at a very young age, where I learned crucial skills that I use in my daily business activities. These people were highly successful, and they introduced me to different ways to reinvest, sell better, and become a better leader just by being around them. I learned that you could simply knock on doors and make a better-than-average living if you had a decent product and a specifically proven sales methodology.

Even as I write this book, I have multiple friends who are writing books or have written books in the past that inspire me to do the same. Several of them have even helped me proofread or given me feedback about this book. And on top of that, my wife is an author! So, no wonder I'd also write a book. It was really my wife, my friends, and my connections to other authors that inspired me to start writing this book in the first place. The positive spillover effect from these peers has motivated me to become better at writing and to push through every single challenge that comes up in the writing process to create this book to help others. These friends drive my success, for no one is successful by themselves; we all need friends who challenge us and inspire us to do our best.

Jim Rohn was a famous motivational speaker who coined the phrase, "You are the average of the five people you spend the most time with." I have found this to be true to a fault in my life. You will become like those around you because those around you will challenge you to be the best version of yourself or allow you to regress. Although this may sound like acceptance, if your friends never call you out on your poor habits and decisions lovingly, they may not be as good of an influence as you think.

Who are the five people you currently spend the most time with? Write them down or gather them in your mind for a moment. Now think, are these five people the kind of people who you would like to become? Do they have qualities that you would like to develop within yourself? Do they have better skills than you? Do they have more knowledge than you? Do they make more money than you?

I hope and pray that the people you currently spend your time with have chosen for reasons more significant than just likability or comfortability. Sometimes, without realizing it, you might spend a lot of time with friends or acquaintances

CHAPTER 9: THE HIERARCHY OF FRIENDSHIPS

who aren't pushing you to be your best. Spending time with people who hold you back can happen for several reasons. You might have just had a knowledge gap on how friends influence your success through the spillover effect. You didn't realize they were impacting you negatively, so you didn't feel the need to change. You might also value comfort more than growth because your friends make you feel comfortable when you don't try your best. The pain paradox would agree that all human beings are naturally inclined to avoid pain and challenges unless they intentionally build incredible habits to enjoy challenging themselves.

Whether you like it or not, you will become and believe what you allow into your life. Again, I don't mean you should only listen to the same ideas repeatedly. You grow only by hearing of new ideas—either through books, media, or your friends—that differ from yours. What I am saying is that you decide who you spend your time with and how those around you influence you. While no one can control you, over time, you will become more like the people around you for better or worse. Surrounding yourself with the right people takes intentionality. You must decide what standard you will hold yourself to to attract friends who do the same. You can't control many things in life, but how you spend your time is a choice that no one can truly take away from you.

Finding great inner-circle friends doesn't always mean you never talk to your other friends or acquaintances, but it does mean that you filter the opinions of negative influences on your thought patterns and limit your time with them. After all, the spillover effect will influence your potential even if you just sit within a certain radius of a toxic producer!

To do this intentionally and not haphazardly, you must create a hierarchy of friendships: start with your top five positive influences and prioritize time with them over everyone else who may not align with who you want to become and where you are going. If you don't have similar goals or trajectories as someone, why would their opinions of what you are striving for matter all that much in your pursuit of reaching your greatest potential?

BUILD YOUR HIERARCHY OF FRIENDSHIPS

Try this exercise.

First, list your top twenty friends and acquaintances on paper or in a Word document.

Now, make three main categories:

1. **Inner Circle** — Your closest friends whose opinions deeply matter to you because you trust that they have your best interest at heart, and they share the same values as you. They have a similar purpose and direction in life. A healthy group of five people with strengths that complement your weaknesses should also include one mentor, who has similar strengths to you so they can help you master your personal strengths.

CHAPTER 9: THE HIERARCHY OF FRIENDSHIPS

2. **Friends** — These are friends you know well and like, but aren't in your inner circle. They aren't in your inner circle because they don't fall into the categories above. They likely don't have similar values and direction, but aren't toxic. Their opinions of you should be filtered, as they have different aspirations influencing their perspective rather than having your best interest at heart, like your inner circle.

3. **Acquaintances** — These people are one step below friends. They can be people you work with or talk to on occasion and are friendly with. Still, you don't necessarily know enough about them to care about their opinions, nor do they know enough about you. These people might move up or down on your list.

4. **Toxic People** — This category includes everyone you know who draws value away from you. Toxic people could be bullies, angry people, overly judgmental people, gossiping people, people who insult you, etc. These people care about themselves more than they care about you. They have been hurtful and caused you to slow down in the past. Sometimes, you might even like these people because they are funny, but beneath the facade, they have negative habits and characteristics that lead to mediocrity.

Now, make a list of the most common people you spend time with on a daily and weekly basis. Where do all of these people fall? This exercise aims to determine whose opinions you should care about and whose opinions you don't. Stop striving to gain approval if someone isn't in your inner circle.

THE PROBLEM WITH POTENTIAL

If someone is in your inner circle, you will become like that person. Stop and ask yourself, is that something you want? Or do you need to find new friends that align more with your values in life? It's a simple question, but it may feel conflicting to implement. Questions like "What if they don't like me anymore?" or "What if I don't fit in?" will likely cross your mind. But this is simply an unintentional misdirection of energy. The better question when finding a great friend is, "What makes a great friend?"

I remember meeting many people through high school, college, selling books, running a fitness company, and being involved in church. Each person is in one of the four categories on my hierarchy of friendships. But how do you determine what makes a great friend? The first question you should ask is, who do you want to influence you?

For example, if you would like to be a person who helps others, you want to surround yourself with people who believe the same thing. You will become more selfish if you surround yourself with selfish people. So, the first step is deciding your values and who you are striving to be, then finding like-minded people who are better than you in these areas and willing to challenge you on your limiting beliefs and give you different perspectives than your own.

You want to find friends with different strengths than yours but share your overall values. It is helpful to find friends who

CHAPTER 9: THE HIERARCHY OF FRIENDSHIPS

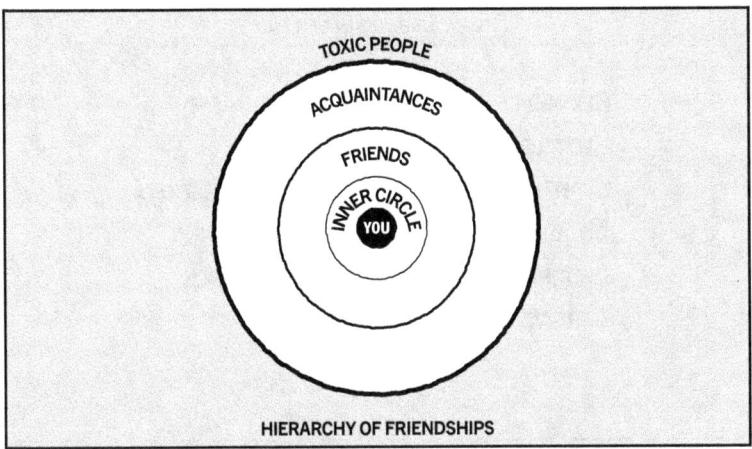

Figure 9.1: This figure represents the various levels of the hierarchy of friendships and the sizes of each group in relation to each other.

are strong in areas you are weak in, along with a mentor with similar strengths to yours, so you can develop into the best version of yourself. You may never become strong in your weak areas, and you will eventually plateau if you focus solely on developing your weaknesses. Spend most of your time investing in your naturally gifted strengths, and you will grow exponentially. Surround yourself with people who see your blind spots and have strengths that are your weaknesses so you can develop your weaknesses to a place where they don't hinder your strengths.

You can make any sort of list that you would like, and I don't claim to have the perfect list, but rather one that embodies who I am also trying to be. At the end of the day, who you want to be in your inner circle is entirely subjective and up to you. My advice is that if someone doesn't embody the qualities you

THE PROBLEM WITH POTENTIAL

TOP ATTRIBUTES IN A FRIEND	
1. HONESTY	7. ACTION BASED
2. LOYALTY	8. CARING
3. FAITH-BASED	9. SERVANT-HEARTED
4. LEADER	10. ENCOURAGING
5. PURPOSE DRIVEN	11. DEPENDABLE
6. PROACTIVE	

Figure 9.2: My list of attritubes I look for in my inner circle.

are striving to become, it doesn't make them a bad person. It just means that you might not be willing to let them be in your inner circle and influence you because they don't embody the qualities you want to develop in yourself. According to the spillover effect, whatever qualities and habits you surround yourself with will become your qualities and habits. It's not judgmental; it's intentional. The person you may not want in your inner circle today could grow and develop these qualities in the future and end up being in your inner circle. This happens all the time because people grow and change.

When making your list, it should be precise, making finding people who embody these qualities difficult. Not everyone will be your ideal friend within your inner circle, nor should you have many people in your inner circle. Most importantly, you shouldn't settle for inner-circle friends who consistently

CHAPTER 9: THE HIERARCHY OF FRIENDSHIPS

violate your personal values and beliefs. Those people should be in another category altogether.

Once you have a template, look back over your hierarchy of friendships. Who in your hierarchy fits what you are looking for when it comes to your values? These people could be candidates that you spend more intentional time with to discover how they will influence you. After careful consideration and a willingness on the part of your ideal friends, they may end up in your inner circle.

Friendship, of course, isn't just a one-way street. You also must embody the values and characteristics of who you are striving to become to befriend like-minded people. You don't need to chameleon yourself; I would say the exact opposite! You need to be who you are, striving to reach your potential in life. You will then naturally be attracted to like-minded people. The hierarchy of friendships allows you to objectively determine if your friends are a healthy influence or an unhealthy one. The only other steps are setting up times within your weekly schedule to be with your inner circle regularly and to remove any toxic influences you may be allowing in your life.

CONFRONTATION AND DISTANCING STRATEGIES

There are many ways to work through removing toxic relationships from your life. So, you can find more strategies than the ones I am about to mention, but the basic idea is that you either confront or distance yourself from the person in the relationship.

With confrontation, this strategy is exactly how it sounds. Confront them about how they make you feel and hold you back, and then ask for change. In this strategy, you are hoping your friend will change their behavior and grow to remain in your inner circle.

For example, I had a dear friend who had just been traveling forever; I felt utterly forgotten, and we didn't seem to add value to each other. We finally got on the phone, and I confronted him with the fact that he seemed to care little about my life after I had attempted to include him in some events and calls. I was no perfect friend in this situation, but I preferred not to just distance myself from my friend, one of the people in my life within my inner circle. We had a tough-love talk because I valued our friendship so highly that I didn't want to lose my friend, and everything worked out! We now talk a lot more regularly and spend more time together. I believe I am becoming a better person just by our phone calls because he embodies the qualities of my list above. He is one of the rare people I would trust with my life, and the idea of distancing myself from this friendship just didn't feel right.

CHAPTER 9: THE HIERARCHY OF FRIENDSHIPS

Option two is the distancing approach. In this strategy, you allow the relationship to weaken because they aren't a close friend, or you think it would be an enormous amount of unbalanced effort to confront them and save the relationship. Even if you keep it, there is no guarantee of a good influence on the relationship.

As you drift further away from certain friends or acquaintances who don't have similar values or goals, you spend less effort on trying to connect with them. You don't avoid the people, but you've realized that the relationship is toxic or unhealthy, so you put less effort into keeping ties with the toxic influence. Again, by doing this, it doesn't mean you are judging them and saying they don't have potential because we all have potential. It just means that at this moment, you are being distracted by them from growing to help others. The negative impact might change if the person becomes healthier and achieves more of their potential. The person just isn't right for you now, just like how you might break up with a significant other who isn't the right fit for you long-term. This also doesn't mean you should puff up your ego as being better than them; it just means that you are going in two different directions because you have different values and visions for your lives.

So, to find great friends, you need to lead by example, strive to be the best version of yourself, and not hesitate to spend time with people who embody your values And don't be afraid to let go of toxic relationships because who you decide to spend time with will determine your self-talk, which determines your actions, habits, and life.

CHAPTER 10

THE BUTTERFLY EFFECT

You have been created in order that you might make a difference. You have within you the power to change the world.

—Andy Andrews, *The Butterfly Effect: How Your Life Matters*

I bet you haven't heard of Edward Kimball?

On July 1, 1885, a man named Edward Kimball was in the leadership of his church as a deacon, and he was trying to help someone named Dwight L. Moody learn about his need for salvation through Jesus Christ. Moody was a shoe salesman at a local store in the same town. Kimball would often stop by the shoe shop after work and talk to Moody. After many conversations, Moody was saved and became a believer in Jesus. He began taking Bible classes and then later started preaching. His preaching became more renowned, and Doctor F.B. Meyer invited him to come to England to preach at his very large church. Touched by Moody's preaching, Meyer's life began to change as he converted to Christianity.

Fast-forward a few years, and Meyer began to do large evangelistic meetings and sermons, just like Moody. In fact, while travelling to the United States and preaching at a service about surrendering your entire life to Christ, he said, "If you cannot tell God you are willing to give Him everything, ask Him to make you willing to be willing." A man by the name of Wilbur Chapman heard this from Meyer, and he said, "He is talking to me, I've been ready to quit, give it up and get out of the ministry." After the talk, Chapman told Moody that he wasn't sure that he was in fact a Christian. They read John 5:24 together, which states, "Truly, Truly, I say to you, whoever hears my word and believes he who sent me has eternal life. He does not come into judgment, but has passed from death to life." Chapman, changed by God, began looking for a partner to travel and preach with. He happened to find a man named Billy Sunday, who had gotten out of a life of alcoholism to follow Jesus. He also just so happened to be a professional baseball player. Because of his fame, he had a huge amount of influence and evangelical success.

CHAPTER 10: THE BUTTERFLY EFFECT

One of the people who heard his message and became a Christian was named Mordecai Hamm. As Hamm began sharing the good news, he gave a talk under a big tent across from where a young Billy Graham worked. Billy Graham had jokingly gone to hear Hamm speak and listened to the gospel for the first time. He was then saved and went on to speak to over a billion people and help lead millions to put their faith in Jesus as one of the most influential speakers ever.

Most people have never even heard of a man named Edward Kimball. By all records of the world, he was just a small-time Sunday school teacher, but because he had three seconds of courage to go and to talk to someone and invite him to church (in this case), he became a part of the chain reaction that led to millions of people hearing the words of Jesus. Even if you aren't a person of faith reading this, how remarkable is it that this small-town Sunday school teacher's heart to help people led to a movement the size of Billy Graham's influence? And without Kimball striving to become the best version of himself, who knows what would have happened with Billy Graham's story?

This concept is called the butterfly or ripple effect. The idea is that when a small, insignificant butterfly flaps its tiny wings, a small amount of air moves. The air catches with other movements of the wind from other butterflies and thus creates a current. The current joins with different currents, capturing water and forming clouds. The clouds blow in a particular direction and become a storm. The storm joins with other storms and becomes a hurricane. Even if the tiny butterfly flaps its tiny wings in China, the currents could reach the United States as a hurricane. The idea is that small, seemingly insignificant actions can cause a massive impact. You make a huge difference, and the only thing holding you back from reaching the potential to make a considerable difference is yourself.

Here's another example of the butterfly effect in action. Do you recall ever hearing about Augustine Washington? In 1694, Augustine Washington was born in Westmoreland County, Virginia. His father died when he was between the ages of three and four. His stepfather in England gave Washington a classical education, and he later moved back to Virginia for the remainder of his life. During his life, Washington was exceptionally physically strong. In contrast to his brute physical strength, his mental strength was his ability to remain cool, calm, and collected. This mild-mannered attitude granted him massive business success, supporting his family to live in a wealthy region of Virginia.

In 1718, Augustine had his first son, Lawrence Washington. Lawrence Washington received a great education, just like his father. Lawrence Washington was an ambitious military man. He joined the colonial forces in the War of Jenkins' Ear in the West Indies with England facing off against Spain. He quickly was promoted to the station of captain in 1740. Augustine would continue to have many children, and

CHAPTER 10: THE BUTTERFLY EFFECT

another of his sons was none other than George Washington, the first President of the United States. Lawrence had a profound impact on his younger brother. Because Lawrence had pushed, educated, and proven himself, he had built connections to help his younger brother, George Washington, develop into a great man.

Augustine Washington passed down his tempered manner and poise to George Washington. Lawrence Washington helped George Washington by investing in his education because George never had a chance to get a proper education. However, with Lawrence's encouragement, George developed self-discipline to study and educate himself regardless of a classical education at the time. The self-discipline and mentorship from his father and brother, among others, led to George Washington's personal development to become the best version of himself. This personal development led him to turn down the offer of kingship over the United States of America.

George Washington was one of the few people to ever be *offered* a kingship. Imagine even having the opportunity. He famously turned down a near-elected kingship for a democratic republic form of government. He was the first President of the United States, and due to the butterfly effect of not only his brother and his father, but all of the Washingtons before him, he became a man who opted to do the best for others rather than for his selfish gain. He denied himself a monarchy for the liberty of others.

THE PROBLEM WITH POTENTIAL

Augustine and Lawrence Washington did their best with what they had, and a generation later, the effects of strong leadership on their part helped a new country form on the foundations of freedom and liberty. Should we credit George Washington for being an honorable man who was selfless enough to deny riches and glory for the wellbeing of others? Or should we thank his brother, Lawrence Washington, for working hard to become a successful military man to develop the connections and knowledge that he taught to George Washington? Or better yet, should we credit Augustine Washington for everything he did to prepare Lawrence and George to be good men before he died? Or do we go even further to the generation before?

YOUR IMPACT IS GREATER THAN YOU COULD IMAGINE

The butterfly effect of one man's good deeds—that you may never have heard of—can make all the difference globally. Take George Washington or Billy Graham as examples; you see global effects rarely seen amongst men. Imagine if Washington's family had been cruel. What sort of world would exist if there was a monarch on the throne of the United States? How would that change the course of history? What if Edward Kimball never took a deep breath to go into the small-town shoe shop to show kindness to the young man? Instead, he walked on by telling himself that, "It's pointless anyway." Would we have had such a man as Billy Graham speak to millions?

CHAPTER 10: THE BUTTERFLY EFFECT

Significant change doesn't happen instantly but rather in a culmination of small acts of kindness and selflessness throughout history. Making the world a better place as an individual starts with the small moments of service and discipline that no one else might see or cheer about. It's the moments when you, like others, do the right thing when no one is looking, help someone who doesn't deserve it, and do your best with the resources and connections you have that make the next ripple start a chain reaction of helping others.

You never know how the smallest moments of courage can have the propensity to create the most enormous waves in the world years from now. The mind can diminish your potential by asking, "How can someone as small as you make a difference in the world? What is the point?" You must fight these thoughts with your knowledge of the butterfly effect. You must take responsibility for your life and the impact you will have.

Knowing the butterfly effect, how can you say that some things don't matter and others do? How can one situation be the end of the world, but another be exciting? Your perspective determines your impact. It's one thing to live in the present and let bygones be bygones but another entirely to discount the value of your current and future actions and how you will impact others.

Try to think of all the small moments that had to go perfectly right for you to be reading this line, of this book, on this specific page, at this time. If you went back far enough, you might remember when someone encouraged you to read, or how your parents read to you as a child. To me, the fact that you are where you are now seems like God's plan, somehow.

THE SMALL MOMENTS MAKE A MASSIVE DIFFERENCE

With the understanding of the butterfly effect comes a realization that what you do, even the smallest moments, truly does matter on a grand scale. The only alternative to this thinking is nihilism, which is the belief that nothing you do matters, so why even try? Doesn't that voice sound like the cynic you've been trying to keep out of your mind? If you accept that what you do matters, then it is time to change. And understanding the butterfly effect of your actions should be one of the most motivating ideas in your life. You really can make a difference in this world, and there are people out there who really need you to become the best version of yourself.

This is why every day is a meaningful gift that you ought not to squander on simply entertaining yourself, but rather, on the betterment of others. The only way to help as many people as possible is through reaching your potential and becoming the best version of yourself. Just like Edward Kimball, you are an essential part of a bigger picture than you realize. All it takes is three seconds of courage to walk into something as routine as a shoe store and encourage someone to make things happen. No one is insignificant, nor are your daily decisions.

Sometimes, you are the brightest light in someone else's life and may not even know it. How many moments of encouragement have led you to read this book? Who was there

CHAPTER 10: THE BUTTERFLY EFFECT

for you when you needed them? Who will you be there for, without even realizing the impact you are having?

You never know how far that encouragement will go. Sometimes, we need someone to show us we matter because sometimes we don't. A small act of kindness can snap us out of a funk of self-loathing and the feeling that nothing we do matters. And just like Kimball and everyone who has led you to this book, all it takes is being intentional with your time, treating others, and actively pursuing the best version of yourself. And time is of the essence.

YOUR TIME IS LIMITED

The key to reaching your potential has been and always will be based on your intentionality with your time. So, why do you do what you do? Why are you nice to some, but not to others? Why do you work where you work, or live where you live? Are you growing, or have you been stuck in a rut for some time? Our society mostly avoids these questions because everyone wants to look like they have it all together. The reality is that we all make plenty of mistakes, and that is completely normal and fine. What isn't helpful is to dwell on your mistakes for longer than learning from them requires.

Unfortunately, it's quite easy to get entranced by life's distractions or errors. These distractions can keep you from living up to your greatest potential. Eventually, you might start to make more money than you used to, and you start getting

THE PROBLEM WITH POTENTIAL

attracted to that feeling. Or maybe you get to a point of complacency when you finish high school, college, or raising a family. You become isolated from the normal relationships you used to have and the intentionality it takes to make new friends. Then the habits set in, and you become the person *working for the weekend* rather than **living life on purpose**.

My brother told me a great story about a co-op he worked at for a large engineering company that created stoves. He was a mechanical engineering student then and recalled a pretty split culture at the plant. He would be working hard to learn as much as possible while on the job and asking for more challenging tasks to develop a stronger foundation for his future in impacting the world, while the average culture at work was to complain about everything. On Monday, his coworkers would say they couldn't wait for the weekend. On Tuesday, his coworkers would say they couldn't wait for the weekend. From Wednesday through Friday, they said the same thing. When Saturday came, they drank themselves into alcoholic comas and hangovers.

Working for the weekend is a mindset that buys into nihilism rather than butterfly effect. Whatever job you do, however much money you make, these factors won't determine your happiness. While money can deliver financial freedom where you don't have to work to live and therefore you have freedom of time, if you can't be happy with small amounts of money, then you won't be satisfied with large quantities. If there is no greater purpose to the money you make, you will float around

CHAPTER 10: THE BUTTERFLY EFFECT

working for the weekend and spending your money without direction, causing minimal positive impact in the world.

William Wilberforce is an incredible example of the importance of understanding the butterfly effect and the massive long-term impact you could have on the world when you live your life on purpose. Wilberforce was born in 1759 in Yorkshire, England. Early in his life, he got into politics and was well-liked by politicians and his constituents. Wilberforce was a man who worked hard and played hard. He worked hard to become a wealthy politician and spent much of his time and wealth on meaningless parties in his young adulthood.

During his early career, Wilberforce was on a carriage ride through Europe on a vacation and randomly picking up a traveler. Unplanned by Wilberforce, they talked for hours about Christianity. Wilberforce wasn't a believer then, eventually converting to Christianity due to this conversation. His purpose changed. He had seen the inhumanity of slavery before, but now he knew that he had to do something about it. People couldn't be bought or sold. They were made in the image of God. He was now hell-bent on ending the slave trade. Remember, at this time, it was likely one of the most profitable enterprises in England. He was going *against the grain*. He had a purpose for freedom. He spent his entire life fighting to end the slave trade and then to emancipate all of the enslaved people in the British Empire. He finally achieved both, three days before his death. Wilberforce never woke up without a purpose. He was described as one of the most eloquent

THE PROBLEM WITH POTENTIAL

speakers of that time in politics. You can't give those types of speeches without purpose. You can't make a lasting change for billions of people without purpose, and you'll never find much joy in life without a purpose. It's easy to get excited when you know why you do what you do and realize how big of an impact the ripples you create now will have.

Now, do we thank William Wilberforce for all that he did? Or do we thank the unknown man who rode with him on his carriage ride through Europe? Or possibly the man in the carriage's father? In the grand scheme of making the world a better place, does it matter if you are the person in the spotlight—like Wilberforce—or if you play a background character, like the traveler in the carriage or this man's father years before raised him?

Like Kimball, Washington, and Wilberforce, sometimes the greatest impact you will have on the world doesn't directly come from you. It comes from the people you touch and the people they impact, resulting in a butterfly effect of your actions. Who can say exactly what your part will be to play? Whatever impact may come from your actions, your greatest impact will come from you maximizing your strengths to become the best version of yourself. Becoming the best version of yourself will add value to those around you. You are making the world a better place whether you are the main character, or the person whose quiet acts of kindness inspire someone to become the best version of themselves.

CHAPTER 10: THE BUTTERFLY EFFECT

Sometimes, reaching your true potential doesn't mean you are the person whose face and name are plastered worldwide in massive beams of light. Sometimes, you are just saying the right thing at the right time to help someone on their journey, creating a butterfly effect of positive actions.

CHAPTER 11

SUCCESS BEGINS WITH BELIEF

Even if your idea seems absolutely wild, crazy, and improbable, it doesn't mean it can't work. It may be so out of the ordinary that everyone must listen to you.

One cannot be prepared for something while secretly believing it will not happen.

—Nelson Mandela

We are too young to realize that certain things are impossible... So, we will do them anyway.

—William Wilberforce

THE PROBLEM WITH POTENTIAL

My first summer selling books was a blur. From collecting no money on my first day to having the worst first week in the group, I wasn't confident in my success. Still, I persisted because I was committed to making this crazy adventure a success. I had nearly no expectations for my first summer's results, but I wanted to make $10,000. I didn't know what was expected. Before the summer, my only expectations of how much I could earn were based on what my sales manager had told me, which was an average of $8,000 in the summer. So, I just did my best with everything I could. I sold enough to be in the top 1% of first-year students that year. I would attribute my success to a pure work ethic and great sales leadership. The following year, I decided to be the company's number one. What grand youthful optimism! I knew I could do better. So, I overprepared, and when I finished my second year, I was the number one second-year salesperson in the world. I missed my goal, but I did win some awards. I had some big dreams, and although I fell short, I wasn't limited by my belief for some reason, even though I had next to zero professional experience in sales. But I believed in myself. If you want to do anything remotely impressive with your life, you must first find reasons to believe in yourself. You have to believe that the potential is there for you to reach. You have to think bigger than average and, to do this, you have to break some belief barriers. These belief barriers are in areas of your life that you might least expect, or even realize they exist.

CHAPTER 11: SUCCESS BEGINS WITH BELIEF

THE SAND FLEA EXPERIMENT

Years ago, there was an experiment called the Sand Flea Experiment conducted to see how learned mental conditioning could impact future decisions and actions. At the time, the scientists were studying the power of belief to determine how the mind could create artificial limitations through learning imaginary boundaries. To do so, they asked the following question about fleas: can fleas learn to limit themselves based on their external stimulus? They hypothesized that if fleas *learned* they could jump only as high as the lid while inside of a jar, then they wouldn't jump any higher than their learned limit, even if it was possible to do so.[27]

The scientists placed several fleas in a jar and put a lid on it. And then they waited. As it turns out, fleas can jump huge distances from animal to animal. In fact, fleas can jump 40-100 times their body length, resulting in about a two-foot jump even though fleas are at most 0.13 inches long.[28] The researchers purposely selected a 8.5 inches tall jar, less than half the length of what a typical adult flea could usually jump.[29]

After a few days, the fleas became conditioned to the jar's height. They were learning that if they jumped too high, they

---

[27] Steinbock, D. *Are You Living Like a Sand Flea? How Our Beliefs Limit Us*. (2021, October 26). Mindful Family Medicine. https://mindfulfamilymedicine.com/are-you-living-like-a-sand-flea-how-our-beliefs-limit-us/

[28] *How High Can a Flea Jump?* (2023, February 7). Aptive Environmental. https://goaptive.com/how-high-can-fleas-jump

[29] Rothschild, M. L., & Traub, R. *Flea*. (2023, July 14). Encyclopædia Britannica. https://www.britannica.com/animal/flea#:~:text=The%20adult%20flea%20varies%20from,(including%20humans)%20and%20birds.

THE PROBLEM WITH POTENTIAL

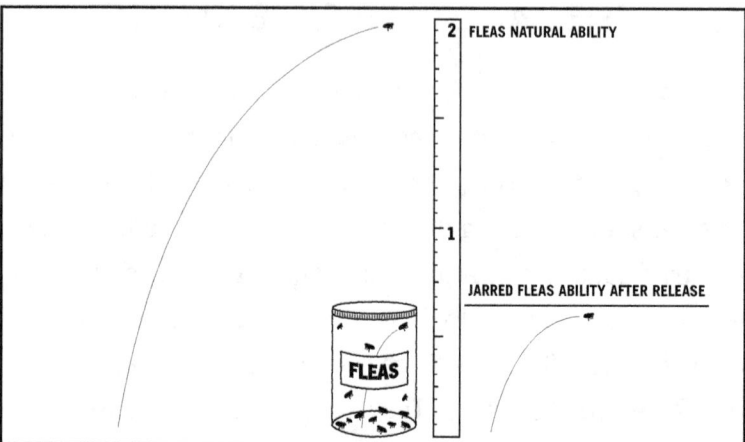

Figure 11.1: This is the difference in the height of the jar and how high a normal flea can jump.

would hit their heads, so they would jump just high enough to move, but not high enough to hit the jar and cause bodily damage and pain. No flea in their right mind would want to keep bashing their head against the jar's lid.

What was interesting was when the scientists set the fleas free, they observed something staggeringly powerful. The fleas, able to jump up to two feet in distance, wouldn't jump any farther than the height of the jar they had just escaped, resulting in fleas that only ever jumped as high as 8.5 inches. Even though they could jump more than twice as high as their previous home in the jar, they never again jumped higher than the limit of the jar, even after release. They were conditioned only to jump as high as the limit they placed on themselves. Unfortunately, human beings can get conditioned just like fleas. The good news is human beings can learn to change their mindsets.

CHAPTER 11: SUCCESS BEGINS WITH BELIEF

As discussed before, whether young or old, we all have these perceived limits that cause us to fall into a negative Pygmalion effect, causing us to lose confidence and put in less effort, which results in a self-fulfilling prophecy. We often put limits on ourselves because we have been conditioned by our past experiences to have limits. We all come with conditioning from our parents, teachers, coaches, etc. But how does this play out in adult life beyond theory or typical school examples?

When I was in my early twenties, I saw limiting beliefs play out every day for six years during my stint as a full-time recruiter with the Southwestern Company. I met with hundreds of motivated college students while recruiting from colleges and universities nationwide. Students would interview for the opportunity to become better communicators and leaders, setting themselves up for future success. I would best connect with students in interviews who believed that challenges are good for you. Often, I would meet these young people and think, "This young person is way more talented than I was before my first summer selling books." For most of the students I interviewed, I could sense a limiting belief expressing itself as fear of failure.

The cynic's voice within would whisper in the student's ear, "What about the economy? Do people buy from people selling 'door-to-door?' What will people think of you? Won't your friends think you're a bad person? What about all the vacations you would miss?" These internal whispers would become crippling shouts unless the student was willing to fight them. More often than not, the voice of the cynic within would convince bright and talented young people that they would ultimately fail if they decided to sell books. These incredible people talk themselves out of trying something new by the hundreds to, more often than not, take summer classes or work a part-time job that they had done in high school. They wanted to stay comfortable. After all, why take the risk? At least when they took the safe job, they knew they wouldn't fail or lose money. But what is the cost of giving into fear?

The most brutal part as a leader in recruiting was seeing amazing people, whom I believed would succeed at this internship, completely not believe in themselves. It was heartbreaking to watch. But I loved recruiting because the 3-5% of students who were just crazy enough to want to break out of their belief barriers and challenge the status quo, like me, were more than enough of a reward for my countless hours of recruiting. Finding those five to twelve students each semester who wanted to experience and overcome one of the most challenging things you could do was awe-inspiring. And I loved seeing these young people grow into a more robust confidence and take steps to unlock their potential.

In my current consulting business, I help business owners grow their businesses by teaching them to sell the way people like to buy. Business owners learn how to spend more time

CHAPTER 11: SUCCESS BEGINS WITH BELIEF

working on their businesses rather than in their businesses by developing systems and a marketing funnel that works for them. I see the same type of limiting beliefs in these business owners as I did in those college students. The problem with limiting beliefs is that age doesn't factor into overcoming those beliefs. What is the way forward? Realizing that if others can do it, so can you. People who have been successful before are no better or worse than you. They just broke their belief barriers through action. Stories help us believe.

For those reading this who might think that it is nearly impossible to go door-to-door and be successful, here's a crazy true story from a friend I've known for years that blew my mind and made me believe.

THE CRUTCHES STORY

At the end of my first summer selling, I placed twenty-fourth in the world among first-year salespeople. Many people outsold me on that list, but one person in particular beat me and blew my mind. He and I worked for the same number of weeks as each other, and we prepared roughly the same way. The biggest difference between us is that he sold the first seven weeks of his first summer on *crutches* with a broken ankle for eighty hours a week. *He had a broken bone and still outsold me, a completely intact person with no injuries*. Even more impressive is that this young man was physically limited for more than half of the summer to moving slower than me while in pain, and he still sold more overall packages than I did.

THE PROBLEM WITH POTENTIAL

When I was younger, I was frustrated the first time I heard this story. After all, knowing that this guy outsold me while on crutches was a big hit to my ego as a nineteen-year-old. After some maturing, I look back on this story and see it as incredibly motivating. I see his accomplishments and often remind myself how results and success stem from within my mind. Hearing this story and meeting this person has always helped me believe that everything you decide to be successful at is possible regardless of your situation or circumstances. If you don't believe me, find someone who has done what you want to do. Talk to them and realize they developed their mentality to break their belief barriers through actions.

Actions solve problems. Actions break belief barriers. Your identity is built from your actions that determine your self-talk, which turns back into your actions that turn into habits. Your habits turn into your lifestyle, which develops mental conditioning. Mental conditioning develops your belief barriers. Incredible stories counteract your belief barriers by offering proof to the contrary of your perception. These stories develop cracks in your belief barriers that motivate you to try new things that you once thought were impossible, resulting in actions that solve problems, break belief barriers, and build a stronger identity.

CHAPTER 11: SUCCESS BEGINS WITH BELIEF

THE THREE WAYS OF THINKING THAT BREAK OR CREATE BELIEF BARRIERS

Usually, you think in three primary categorical ways: the past, present, or future. There are incredible benefits to all three types of thinking and potentially devastating negatives to every kind of thinking if not adequately dealt with. Don't get caught up in supposing one type of thinking is good or bad. Still, you want to develop healthy mental habits and maximize the benefits of each kind of thinking to help you take action to best break through your belief barriers and reach your potential.

PAST THINKING

When you think about the past, you recount memories. Good memories give us an incredible feeling of nostalgia and joy. At the same time, bad memories can provide us with negative flashbacks and painful emotions.[30] Then there are learning memories that are also extremely valuable. What you want to avoid is allowing negative memories to set limits on your potential.

On average, you recall more bad memories than good ones because your brain is wired to remember adverse events more than positive ones. Why? As discussed before, your brain wants to avoid pain as much as possible, which makes sense on the self-preservation side of things. This is excellent

---

[30] Kensinger, E. A. (2009). Remembering the Details: Effects of Emotion. *Emotion Review: Journal of the International Society for Research on Emotion.* 1(2): 99–113. https://www.ncbi.nlm.nih.gov/pmc/articles/PMC2676782/

for learning, but often, the brain can misinterpret valuable learning for developing unintentionally debilitating belief barriers. If you constantly recount the pain of failure, ridicule, and embarrassment, you aren't as likely to step out and try new things as you have experienced in your life already. This internal recollection of bad memories manifests in outwardly negative self-talk that develops inaction and fear. You can see how this could be a problem that can get worse if it isn't addressed. Time is of the essence.

FUTURE THINKING

When you think about the future, you are either daydreaming about a better life, worrying about what could go wrong, or strategically planning for the future. On the positive side, strategic thinking is necessary to reach your potential in life. If you don't know where you are going, getting motivated to leave bed is hard because you can fall into nihilistic thinking where your actions do not matter. If there is no strategic plan for your life, then you will struggle to see the point in breaking your belief barriers. So, you need to sit down and ask yourself, what do I want to see happen in my life? Dream big, and don't be restricted based on the limitations of the average person. Instead, seek out stories of incredible people who challenge the status quo, just like the guy who outsold me on crutches or anyone, else who has been successful when many were doubtful. Write down fifty lifelong goals to get you started, and don't stop until you have fifty.

CHAPTER 11: SUCCESS BEGINS WITH BELIEF

THE DAYDREAMER

On the negative side of future thinking, you might find yourself "daydreaming" (or speculating) on what "could" happen in the future; what you can't wait for to happen in your life so can finally be happy. When in this mindset, you are a "dreamer." The dreamer can cause you to miss out on the joy of the moment or cause undue anxiety. When you dream, you wish you were somewhere else rather than accepting your current situation and making the most of it. Not every current situation is incredible, and many everyday situations are not fun at all. Still, if you constantly avoid facing the present problems that are causing your present circumstances, you could be daydream and continue to be unhappy.

Instead, you should imagine a better future, be inspired to immediately work backward to find the steps to make that future a reality, and act on it as quickly as possible. That way, you can avoid falling into a rut and running the gamut of forgetfulness due to daydreaming. This forgetfulness induced by daydreaming feels like an escape, but in reality, it creates belief barriers that can feel like a prison. When you forget why you are doing what you are doing, you can quickly lose all motivation. That is why you need to strategically think about what you truly want in the future and take steps towards achieving that. You have dreams. Don't hide them, don't minimize them, and don't convince yourself that they are unachievable. Instead, write them down, figure out how to achieve them, and take action. Stop daydreaming and wishing you were somewhere else, and instead, take action to move yourself to where you want to be.

THE WORRIER

The flip side of the "daydreamer," is the "worrier." The worrier lives in the future differently than the dreamer and the strategic thinker. The worrier sees all of the things that "could" go wrong. Naturally, if you are constantly thinking about what could go wrong, you might develop some anxiety and nervous tension in how you go about your life. Chronic stress causes many health problems, and you are too worried about the future possibilities. Hence, you forget about the here and now and how you can mitigate those negative results. Ultimately, you can't control the future, but you can *influence* it.

The same is true for people who catch themselves living in the past. When living in the past, you can recount the good, bad, or learning moments.

There is nothing wrong with healthy reflection of the good times, but you find yourself recounting the good times more often than focusing on the new memories you can create now. This mentality can develop you into a "settler." A settler becomes so preoccupied with all the good memories that they don't focus on making new memories here and now.

CHAPTER 11: SUCCESS BEGINS WITH BELIEF

This seems to be lived out by those who tell you that the best four years of your life were back in high school or college when you were young. You should reject this notion and instead challenge the status quo and strive to have your best year of life every year. The reason settlers don't feel like their life is getting better isn't because it can't get better but rather from their inaction. Inaction causes increased belief barriers, fears, missed opportunities, health problems, and more. Inaction is the culprit, not aging.

THE SELF-SABOTEUR

Alternatively, if you live in the past and recollect all of the negative things that have happened in your life, you are becoming a "self-saboteur." Self-saboteurs are so in their heads about past mistakes that they become paralyzed and overcompensate by being afraid of failure. This fear also develops into inaction, which spirals into negative self-talk, regret, and unhappiness, pushing you into an even deeper cycle of anxiety and negative reflection. Self-saboteurs don't understand that the fact that the past doesn't dictate the future. There is freedom in the fact that your past mistakes have nothing to do with your actual future success other than belief barriers. To overcome being a self-saboteur, you must find good friends who don't worry. You need to find people who take action. Again, the culprit of unhappiness is *inaction*.

THE LEARNER

The best mindset when dealing with the past is as the "learner," which recounts all the moments you learned and relies on your confidence anchors to push you through. This is the healthiest way to interact with the past. When you've been successful in something challenging, you will believe you can succeed in the next thing. If you've swam 100 yards, 200 yards now seems doable. After 200 yards, 300 yards seems doable. Repeat these incremental increases in swimming distances, and you'll soon be at a mile. After all, an extra 100 yards isn't that big of a difference compared to the 900 yards before.

Looking back as a learner, you can accept and grow from your failure from a healthy perspective. Yes, the pain of failure can be very intense at times, but looking back over the situation and figuring out what caused short-term failure will help you be successful in your next attempt. Refusal to do so develops belief barriers, fear, and inaction, causing avoidance.

Both future and past thinkers are trying to escape the present somehow. Sometimes, it's unintentional, and they don't even realize how often they think this way. The healthy way of thinking is through dealing with each type of thinking in a way that motivates you, helps you grow, and inspires you to take action toward reaching your potential. Strategically thinking about your future and learning from your past will help you drive forward and break your belief barriers. When you have goals and visions for your life, you become more motivated and more excited to take action. When you reflect and find out what not to do, you develop habits of success. You need both mindsets to be mentally healthy to reach your potential.

PRESENT THINKING

The last type of thinking is present thinking. Present thinking, like future or past thinking, can be healthy or unhealthy depending on how you intentionally use it. There are optimal times to think about the future and plan, while there are necessary times to reflect on the past. But nothing gets done or accomplished if you never live in the present and take consistent action. People struggle in their lives habitually think in the past, present, or future in unhealthy ways and at the wrong times. It's all about intention and being organized with how you set aside time for healthy thinking that results in actions leading towards your ultimate success.

For example, being present can bring you amazing joy. And you should absolutely enjoy being present! There are moments that you want to experience and not think about the past or the future so you can just relax or be focused on your time. Sometimes, you legitimately need a break from planning and reflection. You need vacations. You need social interaction. You need rest. When you do this in a healthy way you are "living in the moment." Where people struggle is that they "live *for* the moment."

THE PROBLEM WITH POTENTIAL

LIVING FOR THE MOMENT

When you are "living *for* the moment," you are so focused on the present that you have forgotten your past and don't want to engage with your future. You strive to be in the moment, often leading to poor decisions and causing long-term pain. Making constant short-term decisions without any regard for your future and the futures of those around you will lead to mediocrity, and often regret. If you only care about the short-term, you often will avoid the short-term pain described in the pain paradox. You will miss out on healthily thinking about the mistakes you have made to determine how to be successful in the future. Living for the moment seems to stem from running from the past, low goals, and believing in limiting belief barriers, which results in the nihilistic mentality that what you do doesn't matter. But these people are struggling to realize that what they do, although seemingly small to them, can have a massive impact on the world.

As you can see, there are positives and negatives to all three of these types of thinking. To be effective and focused, experience love, and enjoy life, you have to take action toward your future goals based on learning from your past failures and successes. Reflecting on your past mistakes, successes, and the best moments in life helps you map out your current and future actions and decisions. And finally, you must search out incredible stories to help your mind think big and develop a larger belief in what is possible in your future.

CHAPTER 11: SUCCESS BEGINS WITH BELIEF

By doing this, you will be on the path to reaching your full potential with a positive outlook on life.

THE "I WANNA WIN" AWARD

Here's how this can play out in real life. When I was selling books at the Southwestern Company, there was an award you could win called the "I Wanna Win" award. To win, you had to have your best week in sales, one of the last two weeks of the summer. Winning this award signified that you sprinted through the finish line. The physical prize? A personalized all-American-made wooden bat with your name on it designed with your college colors.

The "I Wanna Win" award was the company's hardest to win. Why? In the program, you worked eighty hours a week, six days a week, and talked to thousands of people all summer. As you can imagine, you feel mentally, emotionally, and physically tired after about ten weeks of this (most summers last twelve weeks). As the end of the sales marathon draws near, you start daydreaming about the **future** finish line. Then, you are tempted to stop focusing on the present as the finish line gets closer because you would have worked hard enough already. But no amount of daydreaming would get you to finish any faster. Your thoughts can't speed up time, and daydreaming wouldn't help you maximize the number of families you could help or the money you could make. Once you head home, you're done selling, and your opportunity to save more for college is over. Therefore, you ought to sprint through the finish line. Home will still be there whether you limp through the finish line or finish with your best week. You might as well do your best, compete with yourself, and come home with the best result possible. If you allow yourself to fall into the mental habit of daydreaming, you can become complacent, thus limiting your potential in sales. You will have a slow finish and get home at the same time as you would have if you had had your best week ever. On its face, the choice to succeed seems obvious. Yet, many didn't try their best, falling prey to inaction due to unhealthy future thinking.

On the other hand, you can get caught living in the past. You can easily create a limiting belief barrier on yourself by believing the fraudulent idea that the **past** dictates the **future**. You might think, "I did so well a couple of weeks ago, but I haven't been able to sell more than that week since! In fact, I've just been out of it. How will I ever overcome it? I must have been lucky." You fall into the limiting cycle of the self-saboteur. Living in the **past** inhibits your present actions and puts your potential into a coffin before you even start selling. In this case, you'd want to stay present and use past experiences to fuel an exciting vision for the last two weeks you have to sell! You want to prove to yourself that you can achieve greater goals than you had before. When you do so,

CHAPTER 11: SUCCESS BEGINS WITH BELIEF

you build confidence anchors based on your achievement, lending you strong memories that will fuel your future results. This is more difficult than just letting off the gas, but the pain paradox states that short-term pain equals long-term gain.

In this sales scenario, at the end of the program, every single student has more leads than they've ever had, they had more incredible testimonials than they've ever had, and they were the most proficient at selling they had ever been. Simply put, if they just went and worked harder than the other weeks, they would sell more than they did before. This is very logical. And it's true. Sales, when you get into it, are more about statistical trends than it is about talent. At this point in the program, we had tracked every hour, every contact, and every sale, so we had a proven track record of success. For example, if you talked to 300 people, your result would be thirty customers based on who you were talking to. At the end of the summer, you are the best at selling you've ever been! So, why was the "I Wanna Win" bat so difficult to win? Why did so few salespeople ever win this award? It wasn't their talent, it wasn't where they sold, it wasn't unluckiness. The reason people fell short of their best was due to inaction. They didn't try their best to maximize their time and sprint through the finish line because they fell prey to unhealthy forms of mental thinking.

THE PAST DOESN'T DICTATE THE FUTURE

Your past mistakes or triumphs have almost nothing to do with what is possible today. If you want to reach your potential, decide to consistently compete with yourself to become the best version of yourself. Don't allow your mind to daydream, worry, self-sabotage, or settle. Instead, learn from your mistakes, create powerful confidence anchors that bring confidence and joy, and strategically think about your future to increase your motivation that. What you do now does matter. Be present when the moments are right. Once you've set out to run the race of your choice in life, don't focus on how far you have to go, but on how far you've already come and what the next step is. If you take enough of those steps, you'll get where you need to go—as long as you don't put on blinders or never look up to ensure you are still on the right path.

What is possible today is entirely up to you, and when you focus on using all three ways of thinking healthily, you are setting yourself up to reach your greatest possible potential.

CHAPTER 12
THE COMFORT PARADOX

Courage is believing in yourself and choosing to take action toward your goals and vision for your future. It's getting out of your comfort zone.

—Winston Churchill

If you always do what you've always done, you'll always get what you always got.

—Henry Ford

I remember the first time I sang in front of a pretty girl. Before I sang, I wanted to curl up, hide, and possibly die. When I was nineteen years old in college, I was talking to a particular young lady. This young lady had asked me to sing her a song because I had mistakenly confided in her that I wanted to

THE PROBLEM WITH POTENTIAL

become better at singing. And what a mistake that was. She hounded me; I mean, *hounded* me until I would sing to her over the phone. I was petrified because I knew I was really, really **bad** at singing. I had no vocal control, no diaphragm muscle memory, no vocal experience, and I had never really sung publicly before. My heart was racing. My palms were sweaty, and I felt like I was the main character in the Eminem song "Lose Yourself." I did not warm up, and I weakly sang an easy song over the phone. It was all a blur. I sounded like nails on a chalkboard. It was awful! I had utterly failed. But then a fantastic phenomenon happened. I laughed. I was laughing because I had tried singing. All the fear of failure just melted away. Although I failed, I actually felt proud of just trying. I experienced my worst-case scenario: failing at singing in front of a pretty girl I had affection for. I survived, all my fear evaporated, and I was more open to singing again. It was an incredible feeling. And I had put off this fantastic feeling of overcoming my fear of singing for at least a decade.

I could imagine many people reading this and chuckling at my discomfort. I would agree. It would've been hilarious to witness if you had been listening in on this moment. Even more interesting is that once I failed (worse than I thought I could have), I actually felt like I accomplished something. This was the opposite result of what I had thought would happen. I had always thought that people would stop, stare, and either laugh or cry due to my actions. And neither of those results seemed very encouraging *in my head*.

CHAPTER 12: THE COMFORT PARADOX

I was completely out of my comfort zone, yet I felt more confident to sing again the next time because I knew what I needed to work on. Now, I sing pretty regularly. I've written a few songs I'm proud of for my wife, sweet Danielle, and I've even played and sung in front of my church many times. My progression to achieving something I had always wanted to be able to do, singing, started with me failing and taking my first step outside of my comfort zone.

This is very understandable since we've discussed the fallacy of proficiency, but there is more to jumping out of your comfort zone than simply facing your fear and growing because of it. If you try to grow too much too fast, you can have the opposite effect. Just like your muscles need to rest and rebuild, you also need rest to grow. This rest can often be misinterpreted as being "too comfortable," but it's false. It's a paradox for not only must you work hard and do things outside your comfort zone to be successful, but you also must rest.

I call this the comfort paradox. The comfort paradox is the idea that to grow, you must jump outside your comfort zone and take action, but you can't always be taking action outside of your comfort zone, nor should you. If you become too comfortable, you start to avoid challenges and stunt your growth. If you never rest and are constantly uncomfortable, you will restrict your growth and likely become obsessive. Imagine practicing singing while your vocal cords are sore from singing too much, or imagine not singing for ten years and how that would affect your vocal cords. Rest is just as important as consistent action toward growth. What you want to avoid is biting off more than you can chew! Instead, you should take small, consistent actions toward expanding your comfort zone.

THE STARTLING RESULTS FROM NEW YEAR'S RESOLUTIONS

At the beginning of every year, right around January 1st, there is a massive cultural movement to set New Year's resolutions! It's a new year, it's a new you! Many people sit down at this time of year and set big goals for changing and having a better life. You have so much initial energy and motivation that you can't wake up the following day to tackle all your problems simultaneously! But then, you begin to test your new habits and find them incredibly uncomfortable. And all you want to do is revert to your old bad habits. Researchers have found that only 9% of Americans follow their New Year's resolutions. Within the first week, 23% of hopefuls will quit on their goals, and by the end of January, 43% more people quit on their goals. [1] No matter how excited you get, something prevents you from reaching your goals. But why does this happen?

CHAPTER 12: THE COMFORT PARADOX

TOO MUCH, TOO QUICK

People quit and fail in their goals when they try to change too fast. Their desire for comfort overcomes their desire to change. The solution is to focus on smaller, incremental growth stages rather than try and do everything at once without any rest. This is difficult to do when you have such large goals because all you want to do is reach the end result, and if you're not careful, you will become obsessive and burn out! But you need to slow down and allow yourself to change consistently. The same phenomenon happens when people go onto "fad diets." Someone loses fifty pounds in a matter of weeks just to put the weight back on a couple of months later because nothing actually changed about their life. They changed what they ate for a few weeks and then returned to their old habits. It would be better for that person to lose a couple of pounds a week and to change their habits incrementally so they develop an entirely new healthy and active lifestyle. The same goes for music, work, mindset, or anything else you want to grow. Slow down. Pick one thing at a time. Get out of your comfort zone long enough to normalize that new habit and reap the reward. Then, go on to the next thing.

THE DIFFERENCE BETWEEN REST AND COMPLACENCY

As you implement this new strategy, there can develop a sort of pressure within you to always be growing, which in general is good! Your goals should fuel your internal pressure and desire to help people and make a difference in the world, and your willingness to avoid comfort will help you avoid complacency. Too much comfort will lead to complacency and stagnation.

But that pressure can quickly become an obsession if rest isn't applied to your weekly, monthly, and yearly routine. If you try to grow and never rest, it's the same as working out hard and neglecting to eat, hydrate, or sleep. You won't see any muscular change regardless of how many curls you do. You'll just be sore, hungry, sleepy, and lose muscle without proper rest. Your mind is a muscle, so you need to treat it like one!

When I first got into business, I used to work at all hours of the day. I would take phone calls at night, in the morning, in the afternoon, at any time! If I needed to do something, I would stop what I was doing, complete the work, and then forget what I was doing before. I would even interrupt spending time with friends and family to answer urgent calls or emails. I would wake up and work, work before bed, and so on. At some point, the quality of my work started to suffer. My relationships suffer. My physical fitness suffered, as did so much more. What I needed was rest.

REST IS A GOOD THING

Resting for some can feel like stagnation, but I want you to know that rest is required to reach your true potential.

CHAPTER 12: THE COMFORT PARADOX

When you rest, you can think and take a step back from the craziness of your highly disciplined routine—which is admirable of course—to look at how you are doing things in life. It always helps you to reflect and engineer ways to improve further. It allows you to look back at your progress and see how far you've come, and it allows you to ensure that you are still on the right track.

As I've mentioned before, I worked at a company for seven years, and in that time, I had a great experience, but it wasn't until I had some time to rest that I discovered I was off track from where I truly wanted to be in life. And throughout my time there, the times where I grew the most were right after rest periods. Ever since, I have grown the most immediately *after* I've rested. Because a rested mind is a creative mind, and a creative mind can solve problems you once thought were impossible by thinking a bit differently.

HOW TO PLAN YOUR REST

Now that you know that rest is integral to reaching your true potential, you need to plan out your rest. I recommend doing this annually, monthly, weekly, and daily. What I mean by that is identifying certain periods every day, week, month, and year that are dedicated to resting. For example, in my daily schedule, I rest in the evenings and I have "me" time in the morning. So, at night, I recharge with my wife and recover from intense focus during the day. During the day, I am incredibly focused, so I get a lot done. I feel strong enough to work extremely hard the next day because I have rested. This daily routine, Monday through Friday, allows me to stay consistently productive from week to week.

I spend Saturday and Sunday as dedicated recharge days for my weekly rest. There are occasions when I have to catch up on work, or my wife has to, but in general, these days are dedicated to rest from business. Your business is a reflection of your mindset, and if your mind is clouded by stress, then your business, profession, and relationships will be too.

For my monthly and annual rest, I break out an extensive calendar and plan weekends away, vacations, and other restful times well in advance—sometimes months or even years ahead of time. If you know that you have an exciting trip coming up, you can plan your work schedule around preparing for that trip. Whether you are an employee or run your own schedule, you will still have work you miss, so why not work a bit harder leading up to a week off to rest better? The goal is to work between rest periods, not to work yourself to death.

When your mind may be tempted to wander during restful times—do your best to stay present. Although emergencies may pop up from time to time that can derail you from your planned rest time, you want to prevent yourself from "physically" resting and "mentally" working.

CHAPTER 12: THE COMFORT PARADOX

Remember that to even need rest, you need to jump outside of your comfort zone, be disciplined, and face your fear. Without doing so, rest becomes complacency.

CHAPTER 13
THE POWER OF COURAGE

I learned that courage was not the absence of fear but the triumph over it. The brave man is not he who does not feel afraid but he who conquers that fear.

—Nelson Mandela

Our deepest fear is not that we are inadequate. Our deepest fear is that we are powerful beyond measure. It is our light, not our darkness that most frightens us. We ask ourselves, who am I to be brilliant, gorgeous, talented, fabulous? Actually, who are you NOT to be? You are a child of God. You playing small does not serve the world. There's nothing enlightened about shrinking so that other people won't feel insecure around you. We are all meant to shine as children do. We were born to manifest the glory of God that is within us.

—Marianne Williamson

THE PROBLEM WITH POTENTIAL

When I was in eighth grade, I remember giving my first speech. I was taking a social studies class, and as part of the semester grade, we had to perform a speech on a historical topic in the Civil War. With such a great topic, the speech was bound to captivate the audience! Of course, it was history, and the audience was a bunch of eighth graders... so maybe not. Or maybe that thought was just in my head? I was nervous, not only because public speaking as a middle schooler was really out of my comfort zone, but also because I was homeschooled until the fifth grade, so my classmates all knew each other better than me already. The thought of performing badly made me feel like I was going to alienate myself.

I remember writing out a series of flashcards about the battles, generals, and dates of the major events of the Civil War. I had around five notecards ready for about a five-minute speech. We had weeks to prepare, and the teacher randomly picked an order. I wasn't the first to speak, but I was definitely towards the front of the line. Suppose you've never experienced the anxiety of waiting your turn to speak publicly in front of your peers. You understand how sweaty I was becoming. I had sweat in my hands, down my back, armpits, and legs; it was everywhere. My heartbeat thumped in my ears as I listened to the student before me. All I could focus on was how I would humiliate myself in front of my friends and how they would never want to spend time with me again.

CHAPTER 13: THE POWER OF COURAGE

While all of these thoughts swirled through my brain like a hurricane off the coast of Florida, I heard my name. It was finally my turn to speak. What followed was a complete blur of nerves, sweat, and "ums." I can't tell you how awful the feeling of speaking was for the very first time. I must've stared at my notecards incessantly. I mean, I just couldn't take my eyes off them. I finally finished, I believe around the right amount of time, and I looked up to see all of my friends not caring that I had done poorly. That's right; no one cared. In fact, after I sat down at my desk, I didn't feel anxious or like I was a slimy ball of human sweat. I had relaxed. Speaking wasn't as bad as I had thought.

As I began listening to my classmates, I realized they were just as nervous as I was to talk. We were all so worried that no one dared make fun of anyone in the classroom because they didn't want the domino effect to happen to them. Then again, I'm sure several students were whispering and making fun of me and others who spoke. But after completely failing, I made it out the other side in one piece. I didn't like the buildup, but I did realize that how good or bad I did at this one thing wouldn't ruin my life or kick me out of the pack.

 If you fast forward to my college speech class or even to when I do speaking gigs at businesses now, I experience a similar feeling of nervousness before every speech. No matter how many times I give a keynote or workshop, my brain is still wired to be afraid of social rejection, causing me to be nervous and sweat before every talk. However, avoiding speaking would have massively slowed the growth of my business. My speaking ability, after plenty of failures, is now a tool that inspires others. Reflecting on this fear-based phenomenon, you should realize that fear is something we all experience, and it's something that we all must conquer. And more often than not, we are far more concerned about ourselves than anyone else is.

YOU ARE BORN WITH ONLY TWO FEARS

I read a study once and it noted that you are only born with two phobias.[31] The fear of falling and the fear of loud noises. There are more than 500 recorded fears and phobias in existence.[32] As you grow up, you learn fears from circumstances and others. Many of these fears can be healthy or natural to your safety and survival, while other fears—like those in the social category—can be stifling, unhealthy, and unhelpful.

Focusing back on the two fears you are born with, what I find quite fascinating is that culture encourages you to blast music in your ears and go to parties where you can barely hear anything. You quickly overcome the fear of loud noises when it comes to music, concerts, or parties, but if you hear a loud gunshot, you are startled—which is a good reaction

---

31 Kounang, N. *What is the Science Behind Fear?* (2015, October 29). CNN. https://www.cnn.com/2015/10/29/health/science-of-fear/index.html

32 LaVine, R. *The Ultimate List of 550+ Phobias from A to Z.* (2023, May 17). Science of People. https://www.scienceofpeople.com/list-of-phobias/

CHAPTER 13: THE POWER OF COURAGE

when you don't know where it is coming from. Moreover, hundreds of theme parks have roller coasters and drop towers to make you feel like you are falling. These theme parks transform your innate fear of falling into a thrill ride! But, of course, if you fall out of a chair or bunk bed, you jolt awake to stop yourself from getting injured—which again, is healthy. In the case of the thrill ride or the loud music, your brain knows logically that your actions won't harm you. You've seen evidence that roller-coaster riders survive, and you don't see people fall dead from blasting loud music at a concert. There's no need to be afraid because there is no evidence of actual harm. Therefore, you can overcome your fears with a bit of courage and logic to prove your fear wrong.

In the cases where you aren't expecting a loud noise (like a gunshot) or fall from your bunk bed as a child, it is abrupt and out of nowhere. If you don't react, you know for a fact there will be bodily pain or an opportunity for real danger. There are other fears I call social fears that can *feel* the same way but without the risk of bodily harm.

SOCIAL FEARS

Social fears include the fear of failure, rejection, dancing, singing, etc., and seem valid, but are actually irrational and not very useful in becoming the best version of yourself.

Anxiety, fear of failure, rejection, and countless other social fears won't help you reach your potential in life. In fact, they can be pretty crippling to your success if you allow them to hold you back. But, as I said before, these fears are learned, and they can also be unlearned.

Think back to when you were three or four years old. When you were with your parents, you felt fearless! Aside from sometimes being shy meeting new adults, once you were comfortable, you would just do whatever you wanted to with little regard for the opinions of others. You would dance, you would sing, you would draw, and you wouldn't be afraid to fail in front of the whole wide world or care one bit who's watching. As a child, you just tried your best and hadn't yet learned to compare yourself to others. You just did what you felt like doing.

As a small child, you didn't care that some kids or adults were much more proficient at nearly every task than you were. Instead, you stay focused on your actions, enjoying the thrill of trying something new. As a child, without even knowing it, you were courageous in not one thing, but nearly everything you tried. Since then, what has happened to you?

THE HERD MENTALITY

How many fears include the same feelings of shame or inadequacy that are based on the opinions of other people? These social fears are based on how one interprets the opinions of others, and often doesn't consider the hierarchy of friendships. Social fears are based on the opinions of the masses

CHAPTER 13: THE POWER OF COURAGE

and your general discomfort with others, not the opinions of those who truly matter to you. These fears can and will hold you back from becoming the best version of yourself. And they are developed by your desire to fit in.

Human beings crave love and acceptance and want to fit in with the people around them. I call this the herd mentality. The herd mentality is the idea that, as human beings, we all *like* fitting in, and we *don't* like being isolated. Sometimes, we will keep quiet or act a certain way to fit in that may not represent what we truly think or feel. We mimic the herd so the herd will accept us. This is so limiting because you can't become a leader if you are in the herd, and you limit your growth by mimicking everyone around you. By definition you become as average as you can be so others don't notice you, which stops you from reaching your true potential.

If it's so apparent that "fitting in" will hold you back from reaching your goals in life, then why do so many people get stuck in the herd mentality? Because ridicule and rejection are painful.

STANDING OUT IS PAINFUL

Standing out takes courage because when you stand out, the rest of the herd often notices you, and the herd sometimes won't like it. Depending on who you've surrounded yourself with, there is a very good chance you will be ridiculed for standing out.

THE PROBLEM WITH POTENTIAL

When you feel ridiculed, you feel a sharp pain of rejection. In fact, according to a study by researchers from the University of Michigan, Columbia University, and the University of Colorado, when you feel physical pain or social rejection, neurons fire in the same part of the brain (called the dorsal anterior cingulate and the anterior insula). When you feel rejection, the same part of the brain is stimulated as physical pain. This means stubbing your toe, breaking an arm, or getting stung by a bee hurts in the same way as being socially rejected.[33]

No wonder these social fears develop over time. When you're navigating life, you remember the pain of rejection and failure like an injury![34] If you've ever done a backflip and landed on your neck, you will likely never want to do that again; I can tell you from personal experience. Your brain learns to develop self-preservation habits to ensure you avoid physical pain, and it does the same thing regarding social pain. To overcome these social habits, you have to consider the benefits of the action to the cons of the negative feeling. Whether you choose to do something or not should be based on whether there is a more valuable long-term reward that comes after the short-term pain. And although it sounds

---

33 Cross, E., Berman, M., Smith, E., Wager, T., & Mischel, W. *Social Rejection Shares Somatosensory Representations with Physical Pain.* (2011, February 22). PNAS. https://www.pnas.org/doi/10.1073/pnas.1102693108

34 Beckman, M. *Rejection is Like Pain to the Brain.* (2003, October 9). Science.org. https://www.science.org/content/article/rejection-pain-brain

CHAPTER 13: THE POWER OF COURAGE

very simple, like many other decisions, it's not easy. To understand how you can face your fears, let's look at a fear of physical harm compared to a fear of social harm and do a quick cost-benefit analysis.

WHICH FEAR IS THE RIGHT FEAR?

For example, what if you almost broke your neck doing a backflip? For an amateur such as myself, the benefit is quite low. If I do a backflip, it's cool, and I feel more confident. Maybe my wife thinks I look talented, but if I were to land on my neck again, then I might be paralyzed. That's just not worth the risk because the reward is so low. So, do I do a backflip, or not? There are plenty of other things I can challenge myself to do physically with a much higher reward, so no more backflips for me.

For something like rejection, the benefits are much, much, much higher, and the risks of actual injury are near none. If you are courageous enough to face rejection, you may feel pain, but you will learn to toughen your mind to that pain over time without actual injury. This type of pain is all in your head. It's real, but not exactly real. It hurts, but differently, and you can learn to control it. The massive benefit of overcoming rejection is that the opinions of others will no longer limit you. If others no longer limit you, you can start being more creative with your work and ideas, and you will be unafraid to fail in front of others, inspiring you to action. When you are afraid to fail because your worried people might reject you, it causes inaction and procrastination.

Procrastination makes everything seem harder than it is. Just like singing for me. I had put it off for years, so the idea of starting was miserable. I was so afraid of the pain of rejection that I nearly folded. After I experienced the worst-case scenario, everything changed. I learned to become stronger than rejection. When I sold books, the first three weeks felt really difficult. There were moments when I felt like I was so terrible at my job that I would never succeed. But after nearly 20,000 "nos" in my career, rejection has no power over my decisions, allowing me to take action towards my goals and dreams confidently.

FAILURE IS HOW YOU LEARN

To grow, you must be uncomfortable and be willing to fail. From these mistakes, you will learn and grow. Being unafraid of rejection and building mental toughness will open up more opportunities in your life than simply being the most educated in the room. You can lack education, but be willing to take risks, fail, get rejected, and keep going and still reach your potential in life. Steve Jobs and Steve Wozniak started Apple in their garage when computers were barely even a thing in 1976. At the time, I'm sure everyone thought they were crazy. Jobs dropped out of college. Imagine the ridicule, judgments, and social rejection when Jobs told his peers and family members about the risk he was about to take. At the time of the writing of this book, Apple was worth $3.04

CHAPTER 13: THE POWER OF COURAGE

trillion. Not only is Apple worth a ridiculous amount of money, but it also has developed mini ultra-powerful computers in nearly every human being's pocket around the globe. It all started with action in the face of rejection, the fear of failure, and social ridicule. And there are countless other success stories just like Apple's.

That's a lot of potential benefits for the low cost of "feeling bad for yourself" if you are rejected. Because frankly, that is all rejection is. For one, when you hear a "no" or are judged by others, nothing happens to you unless you *decide* something happens to you. If someone was rude to me selling books, I could have allowed that rudeness to affect me and ruin my day. I could have agreed with them and believed what they were saying about me. Alternatively, I could look at the bigger picture instead, and not worry about the rejection. That man didn't know me, so how could his opinion even apply to me? He's not someone in my inner circle who wants the best for me. He doesn't have anything to go off of other than his assumptions and judgments based on his emotional state, which had nothing to do with me.

REJECTION ISN'T PERSONAL

How people treat you has a lot more to do with them than it has to do with you. People are in their own world, and sometimes, they aren't aware of what is happening around them. They are focused on what is happening to them more

THE PROBLEM WITH POTENTIAL

often than what is happening to others, just like you are. They are thinking about themselves more than others are thinking about them. It's like when you care so much about a small stain on a shirt that no one else has ever noticed, but you internally sweat over it the entire time you wear it. People are doing this with their problems and whatever is going on in their lives.

The people who are rude to you probably just had a terrible day. Maybe their dog died, or they were going through a nasty divorce. Maybe they just lost their job and were stressed. Could I really blame them for being upset if something like that had happened? Probably not, so, should I take it personally? No.

The truth is, you'll never really know what is going on in someone else's life from a quick interaction, but to take their rejection to heart and allowing it to prevent you from doing what you are trying to accomplish would be self-limiting. Should you just stop trying your best because someone else treated you badly? Of course not. If they were rude, their rudeness wasn't really about you. Nine times out of ten, assuming you aren't being a jerk or rude yourself, how someone treats you reflects how they feel about themselves and their life.

For example, during my second week selling door-to-door, I remember being in a beautifully designed suburban neighborhood with green and manicured grass. The whole place had a massively involved homeowners association. I approached a mom sitting outside in the shade in her

CHAPTER 13: THE POWER OF COURAGE

driveway to see if she was open to looking at the educational children's books and apps I was selling.

As I parked my car and stepped out with a smile, I made eye contact with her and gave a friendly wave. I said hello and began to walk towards her, ready to shake her hand, when something unexpected happened.

She looked at me angrily, motioned for me to stop in an almost scared manner, and yelled at me that she was uninterested. Keep in mind I was eighteen at the time, and I looked like I was fourteen. I was wearing a name tag, carrying a book bag, and wearing a polo and some athletic shorts with a sunburn on my face. I was intentionally trying to look as harmless as humanly possible. I was astonished; people usually weren't this rude.

After her reaction, I made the quick decision to go ahead and skip her. Instead of going up, I just walked to the house next door. Upon knocking on their door, I waited three seconds as I stood about ten feet from the door. The family opened the door, greeted me, and I introduced myself and gave them my thirty-second elevator pitch at the door. They were excited to see what I had and invited me into their air-conditioned living room.

We connected over their little one's educational goals. They loved that I was working my way through school. The interaction was lovely! They bought a set of books for their preschooler, and I was off. Before I left, I gave them a card

THE PROBLEM WITH POTENTIAL

like I did every family and asked if they didn't mind posting something nice about me on Facebook. This particular family responded that they didn't have Facebook. They said that Facebook was pretty toxic, and they preferred to stay off of it. I said thank you and went on my way.

Walking to the car, I contemplated why some people treated me well and why others didn't. That last sentence about not caring about Facebook tipped me off to a possible problem. Maybe there was a difference between people with Facebook and those without. By any means, what I did next, I would not recommend to anyone. I went back to ask why the other mom was rude.

Before doing this, I dropped off all of my sales equipment to show that my approach was of pure intentions and that I had no agenda of selling her something that she was clearly uninterested in buying. Even after doing this, there was still an initial two-second negative reaction, but then she loosened up as I explained I wasn't trying to sell her anything and I just wanted to introduce myself, so she knew who I was.

As I shook her hand, she seemed like a normal person, so I just asked her why she was so rude to me earlier and if it was something I had done. Because I wanted to make sure I fixed that the next time I talked to someone sitting outside. She told me that there was a negative post about me going around the neighborhood, making me out to be some sort of aggressive salesperson who was rude to women.

CHAPTER 13: THE POWER OF COURAGE

I was shocked. I had never been intentionally rude to anyone that summer. I was trying to help kids with their education. And this hit me like a rock. I have always strived to be a man of integrity in how I treated women. She didn't tell me much, but it was clear that the post had no substance and no real evidence of me doing anything aggressive. Many women in that neighborhood judged me for being a door-to-door salesperson because they assumed I was like previous door-to-door salesmen, many of whom were very pushy.

I thanked her, spun around back to my car, and started to cry. I never wanted to make women feel like I was overly aggressive towards them. This one moment made me want to quit this whole thing. I pulled my car around a curb to avoid the woman's gaze and contemplated quitting this job. I thought, why am I even doing this? Why am I wasting my time trying to help people when they don't even care that I'm trying my best to help them? I knew not everyone needed what we had, but it blew my mind how wildly different two neighbors could be in how they treated me. What about how I felt? I didn't have to be doing this. At that moment, I was succumbing to the "me" monster.

THE "ME" MONSTER

The "me" monster is a state of mind we fall into when we get into a mindset of self-centeredness. This happens in marriage, friendships, sports, board games, careers, and

THE PROBLEM WITH POTENTIAL

all aspects of life. When the "me" monster takes over, you are dangerously close to making self-centered decisions for the sole benefit of you, regardless of the effect on others. Succumbing to the "me" monster is different than having intentional alone time or rest. The "me" monster mentality makes you despise others. It makes you unmoving. And I was this close to just writing everyone off and saying this was a total waste of *my* time. I was better than this.

As I calmed down, my mind shifted to why I was doing this intensely difficult job. Instead of thinking about how the money would help me in my future or how great this would look on a resume, I started to think about the kids out there who *did* need educational help.

I was reminded of my personal experience with the ACT, one of the college entrance exams at the time, and how I missed a full-ride scholarship by just two points. I wished I knew how to study better so I didn't need student loans. I thought about how many families I had met in rural Texas had children with aspirations of college or technical schools that didn't even know what the ACT was. Their kids were about to be seniors in high school, meaning they were quickly losing out on the opportunity to take the test! College applications required ACT or SAT (another college entrance exam) scores in 2015 and were due very early during your senior year. This imposed a cutoff for when students could take the test that many families were ignorant of. This next thought solidified my decision to stay and try to help people.

CHAPTER 13: THE POWER OF COURAGE

If one kid went to college and their life was made better because of me, would the whole thing be worth it? If I made absolutely no money and people ruthlessly rejected me all summer, but it resulted in at least one kid having a better future, I was prepared to go through whatever it took to help that kid. This is where the pursuit of helping others was worth more than the pain of rejection. Without it, I'm unsure if I would have grown past the "me" monster mentality.

Rejection lost all its sting once I realized that I wasn't doing what I was doing for the people who didn't care. I was doing what I was doing to help those who did care. My focus wasn't on pleasing everyone. It was on helping those who wanted to be helped. By the end of the summer, I had met one family that still sticks out to me.

The family was that of a single mom who emigrated from Mexico to northern Texas, where I worked. She worked eighty hours a week to afford the meager living in a one-bedroom house they rented. Her son was about to be a junior and was starting a job at Dairy Queen that summer. He wanted to go to college, but he and his mom didn't know how to apply or do anything like that. She wasn't familiar with Texas's public high school systems, let alone the college application process. Long story short, they bought a college readiness package that helped them understand how to apply and test well to get the best scholarship opportunities. The high school student saved up all summer to pay for it with his new job. Hence, he had a chance to go to college. This was one of my absolute favorite customers all summer as this family went from not knowing anything and missing their opportunity for school and being able to plan for a better future strategically. This was my one kid.

PURPOSE PRECEDES ACTION

Purpose precedes action. Purpose determines what you are willing to do to make things happen for others. As I mentioned at the beginning of this book, your purpose will determine your trajectory. If you are purposeless, you don't have a trajectory to follow. If you allow something like rejection to overcome you, it's not because rejection is impossible to overcome, or you are too weak to keep going; it's because your purpose is unclear and the "me" monster drives you.

It is beneficial—for yourself and for the good of others—to develop a personal mission help inspire you to build others up, eliminate the "me" monster within you, and face your fear rather than tear people down, regardless of how others treat you. Sharing a kind word with others can inspire someone to go in the right direction. Being kind to yourself will change your life and how you see the world. If your desire for growth is rooted in the pursuit of helping others, rejection becomes something you must push through because doing so makes the world a better place. After all, when Jesus did nothing but

CHAPTER 13: THE POWER OF COURAGE

heal and encourage the broken, weak, and powerless, he was still rejected by the wealthy and other religious leaders. He was crucified in the pursuit of helping others. And even still, he said, "God forgive them, for they do not know what they do." Jesus knew how people treated him had nothing to do with his mission, purpose, or results but how they felt about their lives.

Outward expressions come from the heart; you can't control someone else's heart. You can only control and develop yourself into the best version of yourself. Therefore, if you treat people well and have good intentions, you shouldn't allow rejection to change your personal perspective, no matter what anyone says about you. My intention when selling was to help inspire families to focus on helping their kids perform well in school to build a foundation for success in their lives. If they didn't listen long enough to hear me say that, then that's not my fault. The mission was more important than the rejection, and therefore, I didn't allow myself to feel bad about what I was doing no matter what rejection I was confronted with, even from my peers back home.

AVOIDANCE IS LIMITING

Avoiding rejection and fear creates a box on what is possible, and asking for what you want opens up limitless possibilities. The reward is so much higher; how can you not face the pain of rejection to overcome the fear? Like anything else, confidence in rejection is a muscle you must grow and maintain, and it's worth it.

THE PROBLEM WITH POTENTIAL

Now, imagine the logical conclusion of avoiding rejection. What if you lived your life and allowed other people's opinions to dictate every move you made? Would you ever reach your potential? Likely, you would find yourself getting stuck and plateauing. Because to grow, you have to fail.

Again, if you never fail, you will never learn how to improve. In fact, you'll always think that failing is the end of the world. In reality, when I failed to sing over the phone to that girl, a fire was lit inside me to improve. I knew she would ask me to sing again because she wanted me to believe in myself, so I started practicing. I began to face that fear, and over time, I was able to develop proficiency in the skill no matter how bad I was at first. Funnily enough, I began to enjoy what used to make me afraid. When you face your fear, there is a beautiful process that ensures that you rewire your brain to enjoy, value, and become less intimidated by the activity you are actively attempting.

Because what happens if you fail? There may be a sting, but are you physically injured? Of course not. Remember the guy who outsold me that first summer while on crutches? He was probably in a lot of pain and was worried that his physical limitations would hold him back from being successful. But even though he struggled at first, he outsold almost every rookie his first summer regardless of how hard it was. He was mentally tough and realized failure was necessary for growth and nothing could stop him from reaching his goals, including an injury.

CHAPTER 13: THE POWER OF COURAGE

FAILURE IS NEVER A WASTE OF TIME

Failure is personal growth. Failure is one of the most important things to happen to you in life, and **failure is never a waste of time**. In fact, there is a mantra in the ultra-fast-paced and fast-growing business sector of emerging technologies: fail fast and often. Why? Because when you have the freedom to fail, you have the freedom to experiment. When you have that freedom, the sky's the limit, and you don't have as many belief barriers. Instead, you only have inspirational thoughts of, "Wouldn't it be cool if...?"

Remember, life is 10% what happens to you and 90% how you react. True failure isn't making mistakes; it's giving up on your dreams. Feeling defeated by your mistakes is a choice based on your perspective of what failure is. If failure is truly quitting on the things you care about most, then if you just keep after them, you aren't failing. Instead, you are experiencing growing pains while you take steps towards success.

Failing is a precursor to growth, so a better way to react to failure is, "I'm learning and growing. I know that failure is inevitable; therefore, I get excited about failure because every time I fail, I get one step closer to becoming better."

To reach your potential, you have to fail. And you will have to fail often to learn fast enough to reach your goals. Let's think this through logically.

THE PROBLEM WITH POTENTIAL

The ingredients for success begin with a purpose and goals for your life. Your purpose drives you to want to become a better version of yourself for the betterment of others. To improve you must try new things, which will sometimes result in short-term failure. From failure, you learn. From learning, you improve. As you improve, you begin to see results. As you see results, your confidence grows, and you become less afraid. Confidence leads to better outcomes and capitalizing on more opportunities. As you do this, you start taking more significant steps toward achieving your goals. Assuming the point of your purpose is helping others, then by pushing through your failure, you will help others.

As you logically unpack failure, you see that failure is the precursor to confidence. You must first fail to become confident, then you can achieve great things and help others. Therefore, you ought to accept the inevitability of failure and stop emphasizing the fear of failure. Ultimately, you will fail, and you will make mistakes. Accept it.

Remember, when you fail, you just *learned* what not to do next time; change how you approach the task so you can succeed on the next attempt. Life and success are a trial-and-error game. The reason you grow from failure is because it's *painful*. It's through pain that you change. Without the pain, you wouldn't change. So, it's actually a good thing that failure is painful.

CHAPTER 13: THE POWER OF COURAGE

The problem with culture today is the advertisements and videos of "successful" people who are selling "be successful" *without* any pain. These people are lying to you. It's extremely difficult to be at the top levels of success at nearly everything you could choose to do.

Ask any successful millionaire or billionaire. They didn't get there through being "comfortable" their whole lives. They may look comfortable now, but they are just experiencing the long-term gain from a series of short-term sacrifices they had made for years beforehand that resulted in long-term success.

CHAPTER 14

THE POWER OF PURPOSE

*You may choose to look the other way,
but you can never say again that you did not know.*

—William Wilberforce

Remember William Wilberforce? Well, in 1789, he made his first speech in the House of Commons in the Parliament of the British Empire to support the abolition of slavery. Before starting the movement to abolish slavery in the British Empire, Wilberforce grew up a very small, weak, sickly, and partially blind child. His father died when he was young, and he was fostered with his aunt and uncle, traveling between his relatives as he went to school.

THE PROBLEM WITH POTENTIAL

When he was seventeen years old, he began thinking about a political career. He was elected to the House of Commons and made friends with the future prime minister of the British Empire, William Pitt. As young as he was, he began gambling, partying, and other things common to the political elite at the time—which caused a lack of direction and habitually poor decision-making.

At one point, he and some political friends went on a holiday to France, where Wilberforce went on a carriage through the countryside, where he met a mystery man. I mentioned this story previously, but I want to share a few more details about how purpose impacts your actions.

This interaction is described in *Seven Men* by Eric Metaxas as a divine appointment.[35] Wilberforce had an at-length conversation about Christianity, and after the carriage ride, he became a zealous Christian. As I mentioned before, he never saw the mystery man again after the trip.

When he returned to England, he began to go against the grain of the political elite and focused on reforming laws according to moral standards and humanitarian crises. He had begun to face his problems in life and no longer partied, gambled, and the like. He was a changed man. He read and prayed for many

---

35 Metaxas, E. (2016). *Seven Men: And the Secret of Their Greatness*. Nelson Books, an imprint of Thomas Nelson.

CHAPTER 14: THE POWER OF PURPOSE

hours daily, giving him great clarity and focus on the parliamentary floor. Despite his early setbacks in life, Wilberforce was beginning to achieve great things because he had started facing his problems and found a purpose greater than himself. That purpose was to help people, particularly the millions of voiceless enslaved people at the time.

Wilberforce went on a decades-long campaign to abolish slavery, failing over and over and over again. Despite the countless setbacks, he never gave up. He never gave up because the *purpose* of his efforts would have a massive effect on helping the enslaved people have a better life. His *purpose* in the pursuit of helping others overrode his *personal* desire for comfort. He saw a world that would be better for the masses and did whatever it took, including personal sacrifices, to make it happen.

Although failing over and over, Wilberforce had one incredible skill. He could give speeches that changed hearts and minds, and he continued to speak out against slavery with passion and moral force. After over forty years of political attempts and hundreds of speeches, on July 26, 1833, slavery was abolished throughout the British Empire. On July 29, 1833, Wilberforce passed away, three days after his life mission was accomplished.[36]

---

36 Rafferty, J. P. *William Wilberforce*. (2023, July 25). Encyclopedia Britannica. https://www.britannica.com/biography/William-Wilberforce

THE PROBLEM WITH POTENTIAL

Wilberforce spent his life gladly doing whatever it took to free the enslaved people and stop the slave trade that was ruining so many lives. That's the power of purpose. Even if he failed for over forty years before finally succeeding at his mission, he never got "burnt out." His purpose was too big and too important to give up on. The people he was trying to free needed help, and someone had to do something. I would bet that even if he had passed away before hearing about the abolition of slavery, he would have still felt that his efforts were worth every second and would never have given up. I think his life shows that he worked hard for it, even up to his deathbed. Wilberforce was the final piece of the puzzle needed to gain equal rights worldwide after a long ripple effect that started years prior.

The lesson learned from Wilberforce's life is that however improbable, you can accomplish anything if your purpose is important enough. If your purpose is to be the best person you can be in the pursuit of helping others, then anything you decide to do will include trying your best to make the world a little bit better than you found it. There is a need for every person, whether you are someone who says a kind word to someone in a shoe store or William Wilberforce giving grand motivational speeches in front of Parliament. What you do has a ripple effect. The goal is to affect others because what you do matters positively.

CHAPTER 14: THE POWER OF PURPOSE

PURPOSE IS MOTIVATION

Having a purpose will motivate you to completion, even if you fail or have had staunch opposition for decades. To tap into your deepest reserves of limitless potential, you must dig deep within yourself to find why you do what you do. What is your purpose in life? In Simon Sinek's TED Talk "Start with Why," he poses simple ideas that make the most significant difference in motivation: "Anyone can tell you what they do for a living. Most can even tell you how they do it. Very few people can tell you why they do what they do."[37]

Think about your current career or where you are striving to go. Why are you doing it?

When I went to college and tried to figure out the direction in my life, I did the exact opposite of Simon Sinek's advice. I chose WHAT I would do: accounting. I decided how I would do it: go to university. Then, I would ask myself, "Why am I doing this?" The only WHY I could come up with in choosing my career at the time was to make as much money as possible. There was nothing else other than doing something I enjoyed. On its face, wanting to make as much money as possible and doing something I enjoyed seemed really logical. This pursuit seems to be why so many people choose their jobs or career path. But are they ever really happy?

---

37 Sinek, S. (2012, March 5). *Start with Why—How Great Leaders Inspire Action* [Video]. TED Talks, YouTube. https://www.youtube.com/watch?v=u4ZoJKF_VuA

Would I be really happy making a lot of money but doing something that didn't align with my purpose?

At that time, what was my purpose, really? I desperately wanted to make an impact and not feel like my life and career were on a hamster wheel of ritualistic mediocrity. I had no purpose as to why I chose that career path. I didn't know how accounting would make a difference in the world. I was just thinking of my security. I knew I would at least find a job.

It was only after meeting the right people and contemplating the right books that I finally reversed the order in my decision-making process to why, how, and then what. Why do I do what I do? How do I make that happen in the biggest way possible? What do I need to do every day to make this happen? Here's how that now looks for me.

PURPOSE LEADS YOU TO YOUR PRODUCTIVITY

I am a Christian who believes I should love God and love people. God and people matter more than material things, and therefore, I want to be spending my time, resources, and talents in serving God by helping others. I have specific gifts in the form of leadership, problem-solving, vision casting, and productivity, and these are things that other people struggle with. I know my purpose, and I can inspire people to do what they want to do and find their purpose through creating content, writing books, and one-on-one business growth coaching. I want to see people live life to the fullest! That means I want people to avoid

CHAPTER 14: THE POWER OF PURPOSE

regrets in their lives. Therefore, I need to reach as many people as possible, even if I don't meet them personally. What should I do to accomplish this? I have created a podcast, a foundation, a consulting business, and I write books like this so that even if you and I never personally meet, you might still be encouraged to do what inspires you. When people do what motivates them, I believe they add value to the people around them, and together, we can make the world a better place.

If you know your purpose, you will figure out what career you should aspire to and then you'll live out that purpose. If you have a purpose, you will know what kind of friends you need to surround yourself with. If you know your purpose, you know what type of person you should marry. Purpose is the core to long-term internal motivation that should dictate how you do everything else in life.

THE TOP FIVE REGRETS OF DYING PEOPLE

In *The One Thing* by Gary Keller, Keller discusses a book called *The Top Five Regrets of the Dying* by Bronnie Ware. Ware is someone who had spent many years taking care of people on their deathbeds, and she would question them about their lives, often asking about their biggest regrets in life. Ware found that the following regrets were the most common: "*I wish that I'd let myself be happier,*" "*I wish I'd had the courage to express my feelings,*" "*I wish I hadn't worked so hard,*" and "*I wish I'd stayed in touch with my friends.*" Finally, one regret that

THE PROBLEM WITH POTENTIAL

stood out among them all: *"I wish I'd had the courage to live a life true to myself, not the life others expected of me."*[38]

I would venture a guess that no one on the planet wants to have these regrets in their life. Yet the people that were interviewed, and likely many others around the world, ended up with these top five regrets. The common theme of each of these regrets is **inaction**. If living a fulfilling life is as simple as taking action, why doesn't everyone just **act**?

Action is easier said than done. As stated earlier in this book, inaction stems from fear. It stems from worrying about what others think about you. It stems from wanting to be perfect. It stems from not understanding yourself. It stems from limiting beliefs. It stems from having bad friends. It stems from not knowing your purpose. The common theme within inaction itself is unintentionality.

In every chapter of this book, you will notice that you are asked to focus on being more intentional in a different, yet vital, part of your life. Intentionality can only stem from having a bigger purpose in life. You have to truly believe that what you do matters, and even if you only help one person your whole life, it is worth it to help that one person.

There are many ways to find your purpose in life intentionally. Regardless of the method, finding your purpose takes time, reflection, and life experience. The method I have used and recommended for years is the Be/Do/Have list.

---

[38] Keller, G., & Papasan, J. *The One Thing: The Surprisingly Simple Truth Behind Extraordinary Results*. (2013). Bard Press.

CHAPTER 14: THE POWER OF PURPOSE

THE BE/DO/HAVE LIST

The Be/Do/Have list is an incredible exercise to start finding your purpose. This exercise has had such a major impact on my life that I created a template for you to use in *The Problem with Potential Workbook*. If you haven't yet, you can scan the QR code at the end of this chapter to find the template under Chapter 14. For now, I will walk you through the thought process behind the exercise, which I am encouraging you to do as soon as possible.

To find your purpose, you must first get out of the ordinary "logic-based" way of decision-making and tap into the emotional, value-based side of your brain. To do this, simply start thinking through this somewhat morbid scenario.

Imagine you have passed away and are floating above your funeral. You can hear and see, but no one can hear or see you. Your child walks up to the mic to start giving a speech about your life. What do you want them to say?

For the Be portion of this exercise, you need to list ten qualities that you would want your kids to say about you. For the Do portion, write out ten things you would like them to have seen you accomplish and discuss. Finally, for the Have portion, what kind of things did you have that you would want them to share about?

THE PROBLEM WITH POTENTIAL

BE	DO	HAVE
1.	1.	1.
2.	2.	2.
3.	3.	3.
4.	4.	4.
5.	5.	5.
6.	6.	6.
7.	7.	7.
8.	8.	8.
9.	9.	9.
10.	10.	10.

Figure 14.1: This is a depiction of the BE/DO/HAVE list that you can use to write down your own list. There is a fillable BE/DO/HAVE list in the *Problem With Potential Workbook* you can use to organize your own list.

I have phrases like "Christ-centered leader" and "restorative" on my Be list. I have things like "do a TED talk" and "write five books" on my Do list. I have things like "having a local church" and "at least three kids" on my Have list. What you put on your list is entirely subjective to you. My only piece of advice is this: don't limit yourself, dream big! Put down things that you've always wanted to do. Strive for qualities that you aren't living out… yet. Dream of the life you'd like to have. Be honest with yourself. Don't be realistic. Be aspirational.

As you think about this exercise, the goal is to align your Dos and Haves with your Bes. They can't be in conflict; if they are,

CHAPTER 14: THE POWER OF PURPOSE

you will become unmotivated or not live how you'd like. For example, I want to be inspiring and encouraging. So, I need to pick a career that puts me in a place to inspire and encourage people. Therefore, I speak, write books, coach, and share my ideas on my podcast despite my degree in accounting. I could be an inspirational accountant and encourage everyone I come into contact with. There are likely many accountants out there who do just that, but I could be encouraging and inspiring to more people doing what I'm doing now.

If one of your Bes is honesty, becoming a criminal lawyer may be a difficult profession for you because criminal lawyers often represent people guilty of criminal activity. It's less about the fact that criminals do bad things that you'd have to do your best to defend, and more about you sacrificing your values to succeed in your career. You'll just be unhappy. I am a big believer that any citizen accused of any crime should have the right to due process and a trial, and they should be given free counsel if they can't afford one. My point is that you may have some moral qualms when defending someone if you know they're guilty. So, in this case, putting "become a lawyer" on your Do list would likely be in contrast with your Be list. The same can be said for any number of jobs.

After this next and last chapter, I encourage you to scan the QR code (if you haven't already from the beginning of the book), answer a few questions so I can get to know you, and download the free workbook I after you submit your answers.

THE PROBLEM WITH POTENTIAL

Then, spend as much time developing your Be/Do/Have list as you need. Often, the best things in life don't come in an instant. Spending a good amount of time on finding your purpose now will make all the difference throughout your life. Purpose drives actions, and action is the only way to reach your potential.

Scan the QR code below to download your free workbook or go to **https://joeignace.com/theproblemwithpotentialworkbook**.

CHAPTER 15

THE GROWTH CURVE

*Growth is predictable as much as it is painful.
There are no shortcuts, only dedication and discipline
to achieving your goals in life.*

Jim Carrey, one of the most famous comedians and actors of all time, had a rough start to attain extraordinary results. Before he even stepped foot on a stage, at age fifteen, Jim Carrey lived in a Volkswagen camper van. He was homeless with his family after being forced to relocate from the suburbs of Toronto due to financial reasons. Carrey would go to school and work a grueling eight-hour shift immediately after at the Titan Wheels factory. He worked as a janitor.

THE PROBLEM WITH POTENTIAL

His grades suffered due to the stress of both a heavy work schedule and classwork. His family lived in that van together until they returned to Toronto under better circumstances.

During high school, Carrey began to pursue his dream in the comedy business by completely *failing* during his comedic debut at Yuk Yuk's, a local comedy club. Eventually, he dropped out of high school and started working on celebrity impressions to further his dream. At this point, he was all in. Despite his comedic shortcomings, he decided to make a massive move to Los Angeles. Carrey believed he would accomplish his dream so fervently that he wrote himself a check for $10,000,000 for "acting services rendered" as a future check he would be paid once he was successful in his acting career.

Carrey's first big break was a regular comedy gig at the Comedy Store, where he impressed Rodney Dangerfield, who signed him as an opening act for an entire season. Carrey would later work as a cartoonist in a failed sitcom called *The Duck Factory*. But these lucky breaks built his confidence to pursue acting more seriously. Carrey followed up with several small hits in shows and movies, like *Once Bitten*, *Earth Girls Are Easy*, and *Living Color*, all from 1984 to 1990. Finally, Carrey landed *Ace Ventura: Pet Detective*, *The Mask*, and *Dumb and Dumber*, all released in 1994. Carrey was paid $10,000,000 for "acting services rendered" just like he had hoped for years before.[39] He

---

39 IMDb. *Jim Carrey – Biography*. (n.d.). IMDb. https://www.imdb.com/name/nm0000120/bio/

CHAPTER 15: THE GROWTH CURVE

believed it was possible to do what others believed impossible and, through as many setbacks as you could imagine, become an incredibly successful actor.

Reaching your potential in life isn't easy. Sometimes, it's downright challenging to the point of personal anguish, but the pattern of success and the milestones you will achieve are similar. Whether you look at the Beatles, Jim Carrey, William Wilberforce, or anyone else, they all go through similar steps to reach their potential.

THE STORY OF BENJAMIN FRANKLIN

Look at Benjamin Franklin, for example. His parents couldn't afford to pay for his education as a kid. So, at ten years old, Franklin had to start educating himself while working full-time at his father's candle and soap shop. At age twelve, Benjamin began to work with his brother, James, at his print shop as an apprentice. Benjamin wanted to write, and at sixteen, he felt ready. His brother refused to let him publish anything in his newspaper, so Benjamin wrote letters under the pseudonym of Mrs. Silence Dogood and slipped them under the door of his brother's shop. The fourteen letters were widely popular in his brother's paper, *The New England Courant*. When James found out, he was angry at his brother for writing the letters.

THE PROBLEM WITH POTENTIAL

Benjamin then moved to Philadelphia to avoid the wrath of his brother—even though this was pretty frowned upon, as he was breaking a contract—and stayed there for the rest of his life doing some incredible things. In 1724, he was encouraged by the governor of Pennsylvania to set up his own print shop. To get the supplies, Benjamin Franklin had to purchase them in England. The governor's promise of introductions *failed*, forcing Franklin to stay in England for a prolonged period and work at local print shops. After several other frustrating setbacks, Franklin was able to move back to Philadelphia and become the official printer of Pennsylvania. He would go on to create tons of inventions, aid in the American road to independence, and build libraries and other public venues in Philadelphia.[40]

Franklin struggled at first with some pretty intense setbacks, like needing to move to a different city after upsetting his brother and being trapped in a different country while saving up to return home. Regardless of those obstacles and many more I haven't mentioned, he persisted until he succeeded. As with William Wilberforce in the previous chapters, who failed at abolishing slavery nearly his whole life but ended up succeeding right before he passed away, Benjamin Franklin faced intense opposition and struggled early in life with the death of his parents, moving around as a kid, and falling in with the wrong crowd.

---

[40] *Benjamin Franklin*. (2010, December 10). Biography.com. https://www.biography.com/political-figures/benjamin-franklin

CHAPTER 15: THE GROWTH CURVE

When I started *The Knowledge Gap* podcast, I went through the same start-up feelings as everyone else. The first day I recorded, I felt immense fear. When I first posted and promoted the podcast, I felt immense rejection and pain, as no one was that interested in what I was doing. I kept working hard. I hit a wall. I wanted to quit after a few episodes because I was losing money, and nothing was working. My purpose of helping others pushed me through all the challenges. I worked on learning how to be a better podcaster. I changed the name of the show. I began to post on better platforms for what I needed. I got my first sponsor, and someone finally believed in me—thus, the show has grown and will continue to grow.

EVERY SUCCESS HAS A *SIMILAR* STORY

When I started the Knowledge Gap Company, the process of building a successful business was similarly plagued with internal and external struggles. At the beginning, I was excited and motivated to start the business, but then I was afraid to start. I finally took the plunge and got started, failed, and then had to learn from my mistakes. After a lot of work, I found people who believed in me, and then it began to take off. And today, my business is growing all the time.

The first year I sold books door-to-door, I felt similar emotions. I started off being motivated and excited to start. The job would teach me skills that I knew I needed to build better relationships, grow as a person, meet countless people, and develop better life and communication skills. I may not have known my purpose at the time, but I knew that sitting around on my couch like I did the summer before as a high schooler wasn't going to help me find it either! Only by action would I take steps towards discovering my purpose and reaching my potential. Yet, before I started knocking on doors, I was afraid of failing like everyone else.

When I first started at the job, I sold very little, meaning I experienced a lot of failure. I continued to sell very little while nearly all of my colleagues were selling more than me. I compared myself to them. I made every mistake in the book. I wanted to quit. I was frustrated. I didn't feel good enough. But I kept going… and finally it got better, and I met some families who believed in me. My confidence grew from that moment on. I thought, "Maybe I could do this!" I kept putting one foot in front of the other. I kept going despite seeing numerous rookies quit, complain, and give little to no effort. Despite having people be rude to me for no reason other than knocking on their door, I kept going.

By the end of that summer, I ended up in the top 2% that year in rookie sales. I experienced a similar process with my first team: growing my sales organization to over a million dollars in a year, writing this book, starting my podcast and YouTube channel, and finally, and I will experience the process over and over as I take on new challenges. Are you seeing the pattern?

CHAPTER 15: THE GROWTH CURVE

SUCCESS IS PREDICTABLE

All the moments of achievements in your life, mine, and every successful person I've mentioned in the entirety of this book have followed the same pattern of events similar to Figure 15.1. There is power in expectation; if you know what is coming in the future, you can prepare for that in the present. This is exactly why I structured this book so that each chapter can assist you in your preparation to reach your potential.

Here is a short summary of the processes and emotions attached to each of these steps to achieving extraordinary results in your life:

You start by overcoming the first challenge of internal motivation. That internal motivation is almost always fear based upon your personal identity and limited by your belief barriers. These belief barriers determine your internal motivation, whether positive or negative. Your belief barriers originate from your perspective. Your perspective is determined by your self-talk, who you surround yourself with, and what you choose to allow to influence you. To know how you want to be influenced, you must zoom out to see the bigger picture of why you do what you do, and how you want to impact the world. When you look around in the pursuit of helping others, you will find problems you would like to change in the world. Once you realize that helping others is more important and more rewarding than personal gain,

THE PROBLEM WITH POTENTIAL

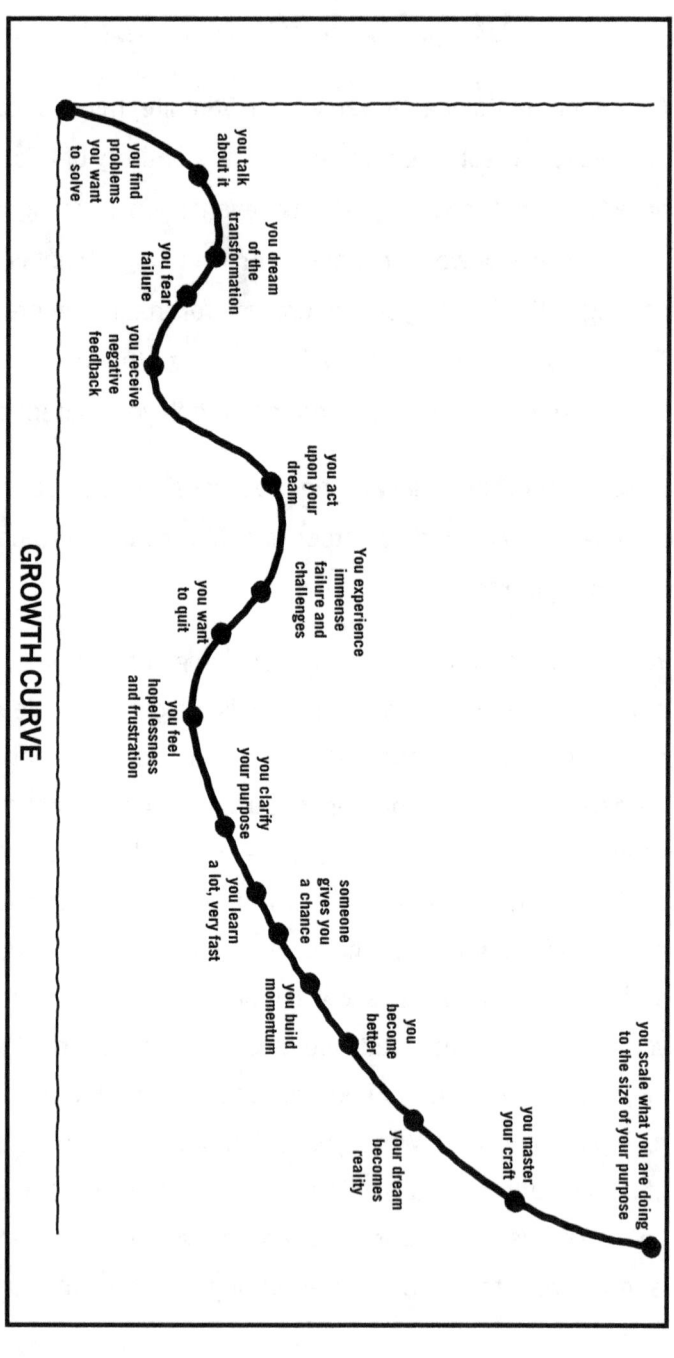

Figure 15.1: This is the growth curve, the steps you must take to grow enough to reach your goals in life. Every step on the growth curve happens to everyone as they journey towards reachign their true potential.

CHAPTER 15: THE GROWTH CURVE

you must become self-aware and realize that you need to become the best version of yourself to help as many people as possible. Then, you will realize you have a lot to work on, and that others need you, so you will become extremely internally motivated to solve your problems with potential!

Once you become self-aware of your problems, you can tackle them one at a time as you struggle to overcome your internal limitations. As you commit to reaching your potential, you will face challenges that you must overcome to grow internally, forcing you to conquer your mind and learn to control it. Those around you will begin to notice, and you will start to run into external opposition and encouragement. You will resolve to keep going regardless to act upon your dream. At this point, you must seek out great friends and surround yourself with the right people who will encourage you. You will experience immense failure and challenges required to start up whatever it is you are doing. These challenges can be anything from educating yourself to landing the right job to putting in the hard work to develop the needed experience to do what you are striving to do. As you are going through these challenges, you will want to quit. You will experience a moment where you feel like you can't go on, but you will because we are counting on you. You will clarify your purpose refocus on what matters most and learn a lot very quickly. Then, finally, you will hit your big break where someone believes in you and gives you a chance. After which you will build momentum, become better, and your dream will become your reality. You will then master your craft, repeat what works, and scale what you are doing to the size of your purpose. From your story of success, just like all the rest mentioned in this book, you will then inspire someone else to journey the growth curve as well creating a butterfly effect of people solving problems and helping others.

There is power in expectation. If you know that there is a light at the end of the tunnel, no matter how discouraged you are, you will run towards that light. I share this with you to inspire you to realize that no matter how long or short your growth curve, every growth curve is not the same length. If you are willing to push through and grow past all of those experiences, you will reach your true potential in life and help a lot of people.

There are an infinite amount of growth curves you can take, just like there are any number of paths to walk through a forest. Whenever you start on your path to reaching your potential—whether it's the first step, the last, or somewhere in the middle—remind yourself of the growth curve's steps. Remind yourself when you're in the midst of things that every emotion, setback, and frustration is normal. The best of the best have felt the same thing, and there is a light at the end of the tunnel. The key is to find the path that aligns with your purpose, and then never get off. If the path you are on doesn't align with your purpose, find a path that does. There's no point in going through the growth curve on a path that doesn't have your purpose in mind. The most important

CHAPTER 15: THE GROWTH CURVE

thing you can do, whether you know your path yet or not, is to start taking action to either figure out which path aligns with your purpose or to take actionable steps on the path you are already on. Stop procrastinating, unlock your mindset, and start reaching your true potential. I believe in you.

CONCLUSION

A father and a son loved spending time together. One particular morning, the father had begun his morning routine, and his son had jumped out of bed full of energy to play with his dad! His dad was really excited to play with his son, but he had an intense urge to finish his morning routine. So, when his son came and asked him, "Dad, can we play?" The father said, "Absolutely! Let's start with a puzzle." The father had seen a map of the world in the newspaper he was reading, and he quickly found the page, tore it up into little puzzle pieces, and set them on the table for his son to put the world back together with some tape. It was an ingenious idea! Everyone wins. Dad gets to finish his morning routine without hurting his son's feelings, and his son gets to play with Dad!

The boy began furiously and excitedly working on the amazing puzzle his dad set up before him. Within minutes, the boy finished the puzzle and emphatically announced, "Dad, I'm done!" The father was astonished! What lay in front of him on the table was a perfectly complete picture of the world. It was absolutely perfect! Every piece was put back together all in place. The father asked, "How on earth did you do that?"

His son looked at him and smiled. He said, "It was easy, Dad! I really struggled at first because all of the pieces looked the same until I dropped a piece on the floor, and when I looked up, I saw that since the table was glass, I could see a picture of a man on the other side of the world, so it gave me an idea! When I put the man together, the world just fell into place."

I wish I would've heard this story even earlier in my life, but it is so profound that I know I needed to share it with you. I first read this story in Gary Keller's book *The One Thing*.[41] This story is why this book focuses so much on dealing with your problems, because mastering yourself is the pathway to achieving extraordinary results in your life. Facing your problems, conquering your mind, and mastering your purpose are the most essential steps you could ever take in understanding where you will fit in the world. Once you do that, you will have developed the antidote to procrastination and overthinking in your life, *action*, and you will have overcome the problem with potential to the point where *action* is your default response to any problem so that you can help more people than you ever thought possible. And who knows, if you dream big enough, maybe you will just change the whole world.

Thank you for reading *The Problem with Potential* by Joseph Ignace.

---

41 Keller, G., & Papasan, J. (2013). *The One Thing*.

AUTHOR'S NOTE

I am so thankful that you are reading this, and I truly hope that this book has encouraged you to do what you are inspired to do. I would love to help you reach your goals in life. You can connect with me at joeignace.com/subscribe for weekly updates. If you are someone who wants to reach your potential or someone who wants to help others reach their potential, call me and tell me your big idea at, (423) 571-4798.

In the meantime, I want to offer you a free resource to get all of your big ideas and goals down on a piece of paper so you can actively pursue your goals in life. Scan this QR code and fill out the quick survey, and you will be emailed a yearly big picture goal-setting exercise that I always encourage my clients and friends to reflect on as often as possible.

I personally read each and every submission and this goal setting exercise is exclusive to those who finish reading my book and fill out the form below. It is *not* included in the free workbook you downloaded earlier in my book. My dream is to create a community that might inspire people to take steps towards reaching their true potential and share resources in order to do so, and you'll be invited.

Scan here or go to **https://joeignace.com/goalsetting**.

I want to include that everything about my life has come from my identity as a child of God through Jesus Christ's sacrifice for me, and that is the basis for me writing this book. Without my encounters with God, I would not have written this book. I give all the glory to God for these ideas. I will also venture to say that God has a role for you to play with your life, and He wants you to be willing to take steps in the direction He is calling you to go. But, if you are looking for true peace in life, I encourage you to consider learning more about Jesus. Jesus Christ invites you to become a child of God and says that you are made in the image of God. You are like a prodigal son who God is waiting for, and He is hoping that you will return to your identity in Christ. I believe there is no better way to find who you are than through learning more about Jesus.

I'd love to continue to connect with you! I would absolutely love it if you could take thirty seconds and subscribe to my YouTube channel: **youtube.com/@joeignace**.

END NOTE

If you enjoyed reading this, please leave a review on Amazon. I read every review, and they help new readers discover my books.

Want to Grow Your Audience?

Imagine a world where your clients came to you and they knew you, they liked you, and they trusted you. What would that do for your business? That's what effective branding and content marketing can do for you. The problem? It's tough to do, especially when it's not your greatest strength! That's where we come in. At the Knowledge Gap Company, we specialize in helping you share your story in a way that builds an audience and a powerful online brand so that you can bring in more business. Not only will people recognize you and choose to talk to you, they'll already be sold on your business.

Life's too short to do everything yourself. Besides, it's a time suck and frustrating. Let us help you leverage your time and your brand to grow your business. We do it all the time.

Go to **joeignace.com/branding** to learn more about how Joe and his team can help you grow your business.

Want to Scale Your Revenue?

Business is propelled by great processes or held back by bad ones. Your systems determine your altitude. Whether it's your sales, staffing, or marketing processes, they all hold your business back from reaching the heights it could be if they aren't optimized. It doesn't matter if you've done 20 years of sales or you're building from scratch; what matters is learning how to build a business that works for you and doesn't require you to work so hard to maintain success. And that's what we help you build. Life's too short to do everything yourself. Besides, it's a time suck and frustrating. Let us help you leverage your time and brand to grow your business. We do it all the time.

Go to **joeignace.com** to learn how Joe and his team can help you scale your revenue.

THE **KNOWLEDGE GAP** COMPANY

Want Your Team to Produce at a Higher Level?

What if your team produced at a high level without you needing to motivate them? Any business owner's most significant investment of time is their staff, but sometimes, you can't focus on the tasks that generate revenue or grow the business. That's where we come in. We help you leverage your time but offload sales and leadership training to experts with over 15+ years of experience in door-to-door sales and recruiting. Instead of meeting with everyone individually to train them, we empower your leaders and staff to develop a culture that builds a personal buy-in from every team member. We teach them to motivate themselves and show your team leaders how to manage production at a high level so you don't have to. That way, you can focus on the things that no one else can do and utilize your best skills to grow your business.

Go to **joeignace.com/coaching** to learn how Joe and his team can help your team produce at a higher level.

THE **KNOWLEDGE GAP** COMPANY

CITATIONS

PREFACE

1 Britannica, T. Editors of Encyclopaedia. *Ethelda Bleibtrey*. (2023, May 2). Encyclopedia Britannica. https://www.britannica.com/biography/Ethelda-Bleibtrey

2 *Tobacco*. (2023, July 31). World Health Organization. https://www.who.int/news-room/fact-sheets/detail/tobacco

3 *Tobacco Products - Worldwide: Statista Market Forecast*. (n.d.). Statista. https://tinyurl.com/tobaccoproductsworldwide

4 World Health Organization. (2023, July 31). *Tobacco*

CHAPTER 1

5 Rath, T. & Conchie, B. (2017). *Strengths Based Leadership: Great Leaders, Teams, and Why People Follow*. Gallup Press.

6 Gardner, Sarah and Albee, Dave, *Study focuses on strategies for achieving goals, resolutions* (2015). Press Releases. 266. https://scholar.dominican.edu/news-releases/266

CHAPTER 2

7 Mayell, H. (2021, May 4). *India's "Untouchables" face violence, discrimination*. Pages. https://www.nationalgeographic.com/pages/article/indias-untouchables-face-violence-discriminationz

8 *Lack of sanitation for 2.4 billion people is undermining health improvements*. (2015, June 30). World Health Organization. https://tinyurl.com/lackofsanitation

THE PROBLEM WITH POTENTIAL

CHAPTER 3

9 *The Nazi Genocide Against the Jewish People.* (2018, October 17). TheHolocaust.com. https://holocaust.com.au/

10 Martinez, K. *Reading Books Can Benefit Your Mental Health.* (2020, November 5). Step Up for Mental Health. https://www.stepupformentalhealth.org/reading-books-can-benefit-hour-mental-health/

11 Rizzo, N. *Over 50% of Americans Haven't Read a Book in the Past Year.* (2023, May 26). WordsRated. https://wordsrated.com/american-reading-habits-study/

12 Mylett, E. (Host). (2019, July 30) *Victory in Suffering—with David Goggins.* The Ed Mylett Show. (Ep. 7) https://www.edmylett.com/podcast/david-goggins-victory-in-suffering

13 Rooney, A. *The Toughest Man Alive.* (2018, November 27). U.S. Navy - All Hands. https://allhands.navy.mil/Stories/Display-Story/Article/1840612/the-toughest-man-alive/

CHAPTER 4

14 *Biography of Nelson Mandela.* Nelson Mandela Foundation. (n.d.). https://www.nelsonmandela.org/content/page/biography

15 Clarisse. *Why 85% of People Hate Their Jobs.* (2019, December 21). Staff Squared. https://staffsquared.com/blog/why-85-of-people-hate-their-jobs/

16 Harting, C. *How Can We Break the Cycle of Focusing on Negative Experiences?* (2022, March 9). Columbia News. https://tinyurl.com/breaknegativefocuscycle

17 Caren, A. *Why We Often Remember the Bad Better than the Good.* (2018, November 1). The Washington Post. https://www.washingtonpost.com/science/2018/11/01/why-we-often-remember-bad-better-than-good/

CITATIONS

CHAPTER 5

18 Louick, R. *Growth Mindset vs. Fixed Mindset: Key Differences and How to Shift Your Child's Mindset.* (2023, June 25). Big Life Journal. https://tinyurl.com/shiftyourchildsmindset

19 *The Pygmalion Effect: Proving Them Right.* (2021, February 12). Farnam Street. https://tinyurl.com/pygmalionprovingthemright

20 The Top Essentials. (2019, November 2). *The Pygmalion Effect/The Rosenthal Experiment.* Medium. https://medium.com/@thetopessentials/the-pygmalion-effect-the-rosenthal-experiment-abc3642de889

CHAPTER 6

21 Rehman, I. *Classical Conditioning.* (2022, August 22). National Library of Medicine. https://www.ncbi.nlm.nih.gov/books/NBK470326/

CHAPTER 7

22 Duhigg, C. (2012). *The Power of Habit: Why We Do What We Do in Life and Business.* Random House.

23 Gross, T. (Host) (2012, March 5). *Habits: How They Form and How to Break Them.* Fresh Air, NPR. https://www.npr.org/2012/03/05/147192599/habits-how-they-form-and-how-to-break-them

24 Rehman, I. *Classical Conditioning.* (2022, August 22). National Library of Medicine. https://www.ncbi.nlm.nih.gov/books/NBK470326/

25 Manoylov, M., & Mendez, M. *How Long Does it Take to Break a Habit? 5 Science-Backed Tips to Change Unhealthy Habits.* (2022, May 26). Insider. https://www.insider.com/guides/health/mental-health/how-long-does-it-take-to-break-a-habit

CHAPTER 8

26 Admin. *60 Years Since the Beatles Started their Professional Career*. (2020, August 17). The Daily Beatle. http://webgrafikk.com/blog/news/60-years-since-the-beatles-started-their-professional-career/

CHAPTER 9

27 Stone, E. *Sitting Near a High-Performer Can Make You Better at Your Job*. (2019, May 10). Kellogg Insight. https://insight.kellogg.northwestern.edu/article/sitting-near-a-high-performer-can-make-you-better-at-your-job

CHAPTER 11

28 Steinbock, D. *Are You Living Like a Sand Flea? How Our Beliefs Limit Us*. (2021, October 26). Mindful Family Medicine. https://mindfulfamilymedicine.com/are-you-living-like-a-sand-flea-how-our-beliefs-limit-us/

29 *How High Can a Flea Jump?* (2023, February 7). Aptive Environmental. https://goaptive.com/how-high-can-fleas-jump

30 Rothschild, M. L., & Traub, R. (2023, July 14). *Flea*. Encyclopædia Britannica. https://www.britannica.com/animal/flea#:~:text=The%20adult%20flea%20varies%20from,(including%20humans)%20and%20birds.

31 Kensinger, E. A. (2009). Remembering the Details: Effects of Emotion. *Emotion Review: Journal of the International Society for Research on Emotion*. 1(2): 99–113. https://www.ncbi.nlm.nih.gov/pmc/articles/PMC2676782/

CITATIONS

CHAPTER 12

32 Batts, R. *Why Most New Year's Resolutions Fail: Lead Read Today*. (2023, February 2). Lead Read Today | Fisher College of Business. https://tinyurl.com/whynewyearresfails

CHAPTER 13

33 Kounang, N. *What is the Science Behind Fear?* (2015, October 29). CNN. https://www.cnn.com/2015/10/29/health/science-of-fear/index.html

34 LaVine, R. *The Ultimate List of 550+ Phobias from A to Z*. (2023, May 17). Science of People. https://www.scienceofpeople.com/list-of-phobias/

35 Cross, E., Berman, M., Smith, E., Wager, T., & Mischel, W. *Social Rejection Shares Somatosensory Representations with Physical Pain*. (2011, February 22). PNAS. https://www.pnas.org/doi/10.1073/pnas.1102693108

36 Beckman, M. *Rejection is Like Pain to the Brain*. (2003, October 9). Science.org. https://www.science.org/content/article/rejection-pain-brain

CHAPTER 14

37 Metaxas, E. (2016). *Seven Men: And the Secret of Their Greatness*. Nelson Books, an imprint of Thomas Nelson.

38 Rafferty, J. P. (2023, July 25). *William Wilberforce*. Encyclopedia Britannica. https://www.britannica.com/biography/William-Wilberforce

39 Sinek, S. (2012, March 5). *Start with Why—How Great Leaders Inspire Action* [Video]. TED Talks, YouTube. https://www.youtube.com/watch?v=u4ZoJKF_VuA

40 Keller, G., & Papasan, J. (2013). *The One Thing: The Surprisingly Simple Truth Behind Extraordinary Results*. Bard Press.

CHAPTER 15

41 IMDb. *Jim Carrey — Biography*. (n.d.). IMDb. https://www.imdb.com/name/nm0000120/bio/

42 *Benjamin Franklin*. (2010, December 10). Biography.com. https://www.biography.com/political-figures/benjamin-franklin

CONCLUSION

43 Keller, G., & Papasan, J. (2013). *The One Thing*.

THE PROBLEM WITH POTENTIAL

www.ingramcontent.com/pod-product-compliance
Lightning Source LLC
Chambersburg PA
CBHW050336010526
44119CB00037B/467/J